To be returned on or before the day marked
below:—

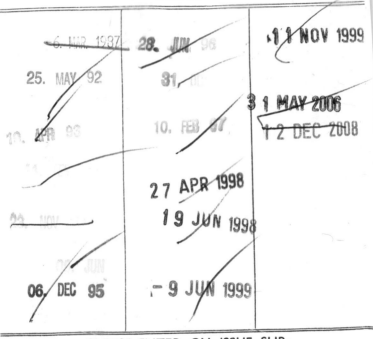

-6. MAR 1987   28. JUN 96   -1 1 NOV 1999

25. MAY 92   31,

                                  3 1 MAY 2006
10. APR 93   10. FEB 97   1 2 DEC 2008

                27 APR 1998

                1 9 JUN 1998

06. DEC 95   - 9 JUN 1999

PLEASE ENTER ON ISSUE SLIP:

AUTHOR   CAYOU

TITLE   Modern jazz dance

ACCESSION No.   56269

Dance Books Ltd.,
9 Cecil Court, London WC2N 4EZ.

dolores kirton cayou

San Francisco State College

modern jazz dance

Book design by Nancy Sears

Drawings by Janet Nakaji Nielsen

Photographs by Jean Colbert (pp. ii, iii [top and right], xi, 128)
Balcha Fellows (pp. iii [left], 44, 138)
Marvin White (pp. 14, 66, 88, 110)
Pacific World Artists (p. 2)

First published 1971
First British edition 1976

This edition is published by arrangement with the
National Press Publishing Corporation, Palo Alto, California, USA.

Printed by Unwin Brothers Ltd.
The Gresham Press, Old Woking, Surrey

CONTENTS

Contents

x

7 ❖ Class Planning, Improvisation, and Composition   129

8 ❖ Music   139

pREfACE

Getting this book together has been one of the most difficult tasks of my life. A primary reason for this is that I have little faith in such a book's teaching anyone to dance or, as a matter of fact, in any book's teaching anyone to dance. I have found myself trying to write dance movements in words, and the translation is not easy.

The second reason for my difficulty has to do with my heritage. Black people all over the earth—and this is true for me despite my own distance of hundreds of years from the Motherland and despite my being influenced since birth by "book" values—are primarily doers, and our way of recording has been to "pass it on."

Given these reasons for difficulty, I have also been highly motivated by the lack of literature about jazz dance and by the misinformation and misclassification of something which is primarily a black experience.

I hope that this book will begin to clear up some misconceptions, especially historical ones. For example, those students who are given any history relating to jazz dance are often told that black people started doing jazz dance after the Civil War, as if the aftermath motivated celebration. Misconceptions exist because jazz dance is primarily an ethnic expression, but people outside the ethnic tradition have attempted to define and classify that expression. As an experienced professional dancer once stated, the very term "jazz dance" was first popularized by white men who used the words to make money.

We should not see anything in a vacuum. Jazz dance, modern or otherwise, is related to the total expression of a group of people and to their experience. The dance does not exist without its music, and to consider the implication of music which places the greatest importance on the expressiveness of the persons playing is to begin to realize the vivid differences between the tradition of jazz dance and the tradition of European music and movement.

My other major hope is that this book will pull bits and pieces of dance together to show the great contribution that black dance has made, especially to the development of musical theater in the United States. In this day of increased awareness on the part of black people of our contributions, other Americans are being informed of the tremendous wealth of culture that is a part of the black man. That culture, including dance, is a continuing variation on a theme basic to all human beings — feelings and their expression.

If I am able to accomplish my hopes, I owe special thanks to those friends and students who have inspired me to complete a project in which they saw value.

Note to the British edition: the records listed on pages 141-145 are American, but the majority are available in Great Britain from specialist dealers such as Dobell's, 77 Charing Cross Road, London W.C.2. The British equivalent of the *Schwann Catalog* is the *Gramophone Popular Catalogue,* available from most record shops.

modern jazz dance

1
bRief HistoRy

In discussing the historical development of modern jazz dance, I face many complexities of definition and classification. These complexities have developed historically with the insistence that all artistic expression must fit into a specific classification. As I mentioned in the Preface, misconceptions arise when someone outside a culture tries to define the expressions of that culture. This is what has happened with modern jazz dance as well as with jazz music. With few exceptions, outsiders have become the writers on jazz dance, the so-called experts, and yet they have only a superficial understanding of the expression. They know only its studied aspects taken out of culture and out of context.

dANCE iN AfricAN cultuRE

It all began in Africa. History tells us that many Africans were taken from their homeland, the West Coast and lower coastline of Africa, and by force were sent to the West Indies, to South and Central America, and to the United States. If we look at the culture of those forced from their homeland, we discover the beginning. The traditional African arts are essentially utilitarian and social; the dance in Africa is not a separate thing, but a part of the total life of the people. There are dances for birth, puberty, marriage, death, etc. Each African culture has its own character in style, formation, and accompaniment—as well as in participation in the dances—but all of the people take part. As Keita Fodeba, former director of Les Ballets Africains, says*:

> The least of our original artistic manifestations must correspond to an active participation in the life of our people. . . . In everything

*Les Ballets Africains, 1968 brochure, no publisher listed.

there is the form and the foundation; that which matters above all in African art is its deep thought which animates it and makes it useful.

The deep thought which is referred to may be considered a basic functionalism in the arts. There is no audience per se because the entire community participates.

In addition to the dances that celebrate the main stages of life, there are dances which fall into general categories: (1) dances to produce rain, grow crops, increase children, etc.; (2) dances to improve the health of a member of the community; (3) war and hunting dances; (4) dances of mimicry; (5) dances to tell of a particular historic event; and (6) dances that are religious in nature but do not fall into any of the preceding categories. Traditionally, each African community has its special artists, sculptors, fabric-makers, teachers, etc., but everyone dances.

Allowing for differences within the over-all culture, there are some main characteristics that can describe traditional African dance: (1) the use of bent knees, with the body close to the earth — excluding those times, of course, when the dancer is jumping; (2) the tendency to use the foot as a whole in that the weight is shifted immediately from one foot to the other; (3) the isolation of body parts in movement, such as the head, shoulders, hips, rib cage, etc.; (4) the use of rhythmically complex and syncopated movement; (5) carrying as many as two or three rhythms in the body at once — polyrhythm; (6) combining music and dance as a single expression, one feeding the other; (7) individualism of style within a group style; and (8) functionalism — becoming what you dance — the art of real life. There are other characteristics that I might point to (for example, the difference in the dances of men and women and which dances are done by whom), but these characteristics are not necessary to trace the development of the dance expression outside Africa.

When the African slaves were taken to the West Indies and to neighboring areas, they did not forget their cultural expression. Slavery in and near the West Indies was not such that cultural and artistic life was encroached on directly. As time went by, European influences merged with the African arts; essentially, though, the dance and music remained African. In some areas, notably Panama, Brazil, and Cuba, almost pure examples of African dance and music are still found.

Some of the African rhythms and movements that developed in Cuba, Panama, Haiti, etc., gave birth to such well-known dances as the chacha, mambo, pachanga, merengue, and samba. In addition to these social dances there developed essentially African dances that are religious in nature. In Haiti, for example, the Vodun worshippers honored the African gods Dumballa, Shango, and the like. In the Vodun ceremonies, each god has his own rhythms and dance steps. These dances have the specific characteristics of African dance.

Wherever slaves were taken in South and Central America and in the West Indies, African dance appeared somewhat out of context — sometimes tied in with Christianity and sometimes merged with other European influences, but nonetheless still one step from its roots in traditional African dance. In the United States, though, African dance did not survive so easily.

black dance in the United States

History tells us that the slavery endured in the United States by black people was worse than any other slavery in the history of mankind. Not only was enslavement a horror, but in a land where so many values and points of view were dissimilar, all aspects of African life were ridiculed or destroyed. The areas that were hardest for the alien culture to reach were those of dance and music, as these could be maintained informally in many settings. The slavemasters tried to eliminate such cultural expression in the slaves by prohibiting the playing of drums and any gatherings in large groups up until 1812. However, the slavemasters were unable to destroy African dance and music completely. As the great anthropologist Pearl Primus recalls *:

> On my trips south of the Mason and Dixon line in 1944 I discovered in the Baptist Churches the voice of the drum — not in any instrument, but in the throat of the preacher. I found the dynamic sweep of movement through space (so characteristic of Africa) in the motions of minister and congregation alike. I felt in the sermons the crashing thunder dances of Africa and I was hypnotized by the pounding

* Chujoy, Anatole, and Manchester, P. W. *Dance Encyclopedia*. New York: Simon and Schuster, 1967, pp. 387-89.

rhythm of song. Did the dance which the slaves brought to America and which disappeared under pressure of their masters break through disguised in the freedom of their church? . . . Dancing in the churches of the South, though it is not called dance, resembles what I know of Africa so closely, I can say with conviction that the people brought here centuries ago from the Gold Coast and other parts of West Africa preserved the dance in their religious expression.

When the drums were prohibited, slaves found replacements: bone clappers, banjos, and hands and feet. Both in places like Congo Square, an area just outside New Orleans where slaves congregated, and in the churches, the traditions of dance were revived and carried on. Whether in the circle dances of Congo Square or in the religious movements called anything but dance (for dance was considered sinful), the characteristics remained: (1) bent knees, with the body close to the earth; (2) tendency toward use of the whole foot and immediate transfer of weight; (3) isolation of body parts in movement; (4) rhythmically complex and syncopated movement; (5) carrying as many as two or three rhythms in the body at once – polyrhythm; (6) music and dance as a single expression; (7) individualism of style within a group style; and (8) functionalism – becoming what you dance – the art of real life.

Given all the influences of slavery in a foreign land with basic differences in life values, another characteristic emerged as a matter of necessity, and that was a richness of ways of dance expression, a variety of modes to reach the same artistic goal. In trying to erase all cultural expression, the slavemaster only encouraged that expression to happen in different ways, and hence the development of dance movement through blues, spirituals, gospel songs, so-called shuffles, hoe-downs, etc. I do not mean to say that prior to this time there was no creativity within traditional African dance; rather, new modes of dance expression were highly emphasized given the situation of the slave. Of the two settings, the church and the social gathering, the church has remained much more traditional in terms of African dance – free almost entirely from other influences. This is true especially in the churches of the South, where all of life is more traditional.

The European influences on the dance expression of the slaves came through reels, quadrilles, clogs, etc.; in other words, the influences were primarily specific steps from European folk sources. When the traditional African characteristics of rhythmic complexity and syncopation were combined with some of the movements of the European folk dances, the first development was tap dance in the mid-1800's. More precisely, tap dance was the earliest tangible development we are aware of. I am sure that hundreds of other developments occurred which were never popularized or seen by whites and that therefore were not institutionalized in any way. The point about the institutionalization of dance is an important one. The beginnings of jazz dance for many people equalled its appearance on stage. For these people, the dance did not exist until it had gained the sanction of a socially accepted white institution.

public peRfoRmaNce: miNstRel shows aNd vaudeville

When the minstrel shows got underway, more people became familiar with the black dance culture, although in the beginning it was through white performers in blackface. Although the minstrel shows were based on the life of black people, most of the early minstrel companies that appeared on stage, such as the Virginia Minstrels and the Ethiopian Minstrels, were white. In general, blacks were not permitted on stage. Before the Civil War, hundreds of white minstrels appeared in burnt cork, imitating the black man's speech, telling his jokes, and singing his songs. They mimicked the dances of the black field hands and the cake-walks of the house servants. The plantation stick dance became a standard comedy number.*

Even though blacks were not permitted to perform in early minstrel shows, they did perform in medicine shows, carnivals, circuses, and the like. After the Civil War, the situation remained essentially the same. As history has consistently indicated, the only time black performers were allowed to perform commercially in the United States was when it was not economically profitable for whites to do so. Even though the minstrel show was the most popular form of entertainment in the United States from about 1845 to about 1900, few black companies

---

*Hughes, Langston, and Meltzer, M. *Black Magic: A Pictorial History of the Negro in American Entertainment.* Englewood Cliffs, N.J.: Prentice-Hall, 1967, p. 28.

existed. Because of the competition of the white companies, black minstrel troupes — including "The South Before the War," "The Creole
Show," and "Oriental America" — found that the only way talent could
be sold was to give people what they wanted to see: a stereotyped black
who made fun of himself and his culture.

During the early 1900s, more and more blacks were able to perform
outside the narrow stereotype of·the minstrel show. Traveling shows
spread the music and dance culture of black people far and wide. In
addition to the spreading of culture, another important development
was taking place: the beginning of the musical theater.

Meanwhile, another theatrical form was becoming popular: vaudeville. Innumerable black performers did comedy, song and dance
sketches, and musical revues in vaudeville shows. This was a time when
slapstick comedy came to the fore. A busy black circuit, the Theater
Owners' Booking Association (T.O.B.A.), gave black entertainers an
opportunity to gain theatrical experience without having to please
white audiences and white theater managers. Headliners for T.O.B.A.
included Butterbeans and Susie, who used a cakewalk and an eccentric
dance in their comedy act, and the tap-dancing Whitman sisters. Meanwhile, white audiences selected some of the black performers as favor-
ites, as a matter of exceptional interest. In these cases, the artists would
travel the white circuit as well as the black.

developments in social dance

During the early 1900s, another development took place: the social
dance that came out of the everyday life of black people became extremely popular with the white population as a whole. Through the
years, dance had remained an important part of the expression of black
people in church and at social gatherings, and social dance, or "ver-
nacular dance" as Marshall Stearns calls it,* continued to be more important than any one form that evolved out of it. Even when the dance
of the musical revue evolved, it was still directly associated with and
tied to the everyday dance of the people.

* Stearns, Marshall, and Stearns, Jean. *Jazz Dance*. New York: Macmillan, 1968.

The Nicholas Brothers in "St. Louis Woman," a black musical play which opened in New York in 1946.

Bill Robinson and Eleanor Powell in an impromptu dance at the Cotton Club in 1938.

Avon Long as Sportin' Life in a "Porgy and Bess" revival, 1942.

Katherine Dunham with her dancers in a Haitian dance from "Tropical Revue."

Many of the popular dances presented the art of real life that goes back to Africa: the Turkey Trot, Grizzly Bear, Monkey, Chicken Scratch, Bullfrog Hop, Kangaroo Dip, Bunny Hug, etc. In the 1920's, the Charleston caught on and spread throughout the world. This dance sparked participation and interest such as had never been seen before in the United States or Europe. I am sure that most black people were puzzled as to why the Charleston became so popular. Let me return for a moment to the foundation of arts in Africa. The arts there were part of the total complex of life; there was no audience, and everyone participated in dance and music in some way. Even though black Americans had lived through hundreds of years of slavery, the role of the arts in life carried over to a degree. Everyone participated at home, in church, and at parties and gatherings. In contrast, white Americans participated occasionally in group dances such as the square dance or in more formal social dances such as the waltz which were derivations of court dances, or they did not participate at all. The Charleston, along with the Black Bottom and the Shim Sham Shimmy in the 1920's and the Lindy Hop in the 1930's, radically changed the social dance patterns of the white community.

developments in stage dance

The first four decades of this century were also a thriving time for black dancers on stage. Such greats as Bill "Bojangles" Robinson, Bert Williams, the Nicholas Brothers, the Berry Brothers, and Buck and Bubbles were in the heyday of performing. Nightclubs in Harlem opened up more possibilities for performers. There are few black people over the age of forty who are not familiar with the association of the Cotton Club, Harlem, and jazz music in the 1920's and 1930's, as well as the performers who appeared there.

The opening of a show called "Shuffle Along" in 1921 began a decade of black shows downtown, on Broadway. Again, this popularity exposed more and more whites to black music, dance, and comedy. Many of these shows also traveled to Europe and were highly successful there. Some of the best-known dancers at the time were Earl "Snake Hips" Tucker, Avon Long, and Baby Alice Whitman.

As black dance became more popular on stage, it was influenced by the tastes of white audiences. What grew out of the everyday life of one culture was modified to appeal to an audience outside the culture, and black theatrical dance ceased to be tied so closely to everyday dance expression. The characteristics of African dance were and are still the basic characteristics of dance in the black churches and social gatherings of the masses of black Americans. But with the development of black music and dance on stage in the 1920's, performance and everyday participation became separate.

The term "jazz dance" probably appeared at this time, the "jazz age." But jazz dance is *not* limited to the social or stage dances of the 1920's. The definition of jazz dance must include the entire dance culture, or the term has little meaning. This fact is especially important because, following the oral tradition of African life, black Americans did not write down their cultural expressions in general—they did a thing as opposed to writing about it or classifying it. White Americans, however, tend to classify an item and put it in an appropriate compartment. They tend toward a "dissecting out" approach to all things.

It was during the 1920's that authentic black musical expression, like black social dance, became separate from the dance as performed on the stage. This development is interesting because it signals the Americanization of black expression in music and dance for whites. The Americanization occurred through white influence, which was mainly economic. All too often art became a matter of "selling the product."

The popularity of the black musical theater lasted a decade, and its impact revolutionized concepts of music, dance, and theater in America. The coming of the Depression and the Americanization of jazz dance were the major forces that brought an end to the "high time" in black musical theater. The end of the theater naturally coincided with the development of musical theater as a whole, which means that from the 1930's onward the emphasis has been on white musical theater. Although most of the dancing that used to be called "chorus" or theatrical was learned by white performers who studied with black teachers, after the 1920's black dancers were no longer used on Broadway except for such highly specialized performers as Bill Robinson or the Nicholas Brothers, and usually these performers appeared in a limited "spot" in a production.

Talley Beatty

Donald MacKayle

Pacific World Artists

Pacific World Artists

Eleo Pomare

The Eleo Pomare Dance Company

In 1931, when the New Negro Art Theatre presented a recital that included a suite of interpretive dance based on Southern spirituals, old limitations were defied and a precedent was established. A pioneer black dancer in the interpretive field, Hemsely Winfield, was the moving spirit behind the program. The suite dealt with an area of black life that had never before been presented through dance on the stage. Both the subject matter and the approach of the dance went beyond the scope of black dance tradition, and in so doing the suite set a precedent for future interpretive presentations of black music and dance.

Since then there has been a continuing evolution of jazz-oriented dance in the theater, movies, television, dance studios, and on the concert stage. Innumerable dancers and choreographers have contributed to this evolution. Pearl Primus, Katherine Dunham, Walter Nicks, Talley Beatty, Eleo Pomare, Jack Cole, Alvin Ailey, JoJo Smith, Donald MacKayle, and Syvilla Forte are among the many artists who have brought jazz dance to the varied media and locations in which we find it today.

Alvin Ailey

2

WARM—UP EXERCISES

This book is arranged so that the technique begins quite simply and progresses to difficult exercises. In this chapter the prime concern is to get the body warmed up and moving. The second concern is to increase flexibility and strength throughout the body, and the third is to increase the realm of movement possibilities for each body.

The amount of time that should be spent on any one technique is up to the instructor. However, I suggest that all body parts should be warmed up slowly before going into any vigorous movement. I also suggest that it is not wise to spend too much time on any one body part working in a particular way – for example the abdomen doing many small contractions and releases, or the legs doing many repetitions of pliés on half toe.

Although each student should be concerned with developing a greater stretch or a higher extension, I believe the time has come when the teacher should encourage the student to concentrate on his own body in the technique and not on the technique solely. The student should be made aware of his own body and what it can do, given its anatomical structure. What is important is learning movement through positions, as opposed to the learning of positions for their own sake. This stress on individual capabilities and on movement through positions is probably more important in jazz dance than in other forms of dance. After all, the student of jazz dance should strive for technical facility only as a means to his own expression.

How the content of this chapter should be used in class work is discussed in Chapter 7.

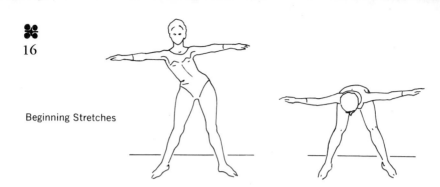

Beginning Stretches

bEGINNING STRETCHES

Stand in a wide second position — that is, with the feet far apart and turned out, the arms in second position (directly to the sides), and the palms toward the floor.

Count 1-8   Stretch directly to the right side through the upper body and the right arm, and at the same time release the left hip to the left. (See the illustration.)

Count 1-8   Stretch directly to the left side through the upper body and the left arm, and at the same time release the right hip to the right.

Count 1-8   Lift the chest diagonally upward and forward, lift the head so as to focus diagonally toward the ceiling, and then stretch upward and forward through the chest until the back is parallel to the floor and the face is toward the floor. Keep the arms in second position. (See the illustration.)

Note: Between each of the stretches, bring the body back to center and then stretch again. When stretching to either side, be sure the upper body does not pull diagonally forward. When lifting the chest, be sure there is no arching of the lower back.

Repeat these stretches in each direction for six counts, then four counts, two counts, and one count. Then repeat the stretches four times, taking one count in each direction.

pliÉ EXERCISE 1

Stand in first position parallel — that is, with the feet parallel but not quite touching and the arms neutral (hanging relaxed at the sides).

Count 1   Plié, keeping the heels on the floor.

2   Straighten the knees.

3   Lift the heels away from the floor to stand on half toe.

4   Lower the heels to the floor.

Repeat three times.

Count 1   Lift the heels to stand on half toe.

     2   Plié without lowering the heels.

     3   Lower the heels to the floor, keeping the knees in place.

     4   Straighten the knees.

      Repeat three times.

Combine the two pliés above in the following manner:

Count 1   Plié, keeping the heels on the floor.

     2   Straighten the knees.

     3   Lift the heels to stand on half toe.

     4   Lower the heels to the floor.

     5   Lift the heels to stand on half toe.

     6   Plié without lowering the heels.

     7   Lower the heels to the floor, keeping the knees in place.

     8   Straighten the knees.

plié EXERCISE 2

Stand with the feet parallel but not quite touching. Keeping the knees in place, round the back and move the head toward the knees. Hold the entire hand — including the fingertips — straight, and reach for the floor a few inches in front of the toes.

Count 1   Plié, keeping the heels and the fingertips on the floor.

     2   Straighten the knees.

     3   Lift the heels away from the floor.

     4   Lower the heels to the floor.

      Repeat three times.

Note: On count 3, avoid shifting the body weight forward.

Do this exercise four times in second position parallel — that is, with the feet parallel and twelve to twenty-four inches apart and the arms extended directly to the sides. Then do the exercise four times in regular first position — with the feet turned out — and four times in regular second position — again, with the feet turned out.

plié EXERCISE 3

Stand in first position parallel.

Count 1   Plié, keeping the heels on the floor.

2   Straighten the knees. At the same time, bend the upper body forward until it is parallel to the floor and swing the arms forward and down until they are in front, parallel to the floor and with the palms toward the floor.

3   Plié, return the upper body to center as in count 1, and return the arms to neutral as in count 1.

4   Straighten the knees.

Repeat at least three times.

Note: On count 2, be sure the armswing and the straightening of the knees are done simultaneously.

Do this exercise four times in second position parallel.

Count 1   Plié deep so that the heels go off the floor.

2   Straighten the knees. At the same time, bend the upper body forward until it is parallel to the floor and swing the arms forward and down until they are in front, parallel to the floor and with the palms toward the floor.

3   Plié deep so that the heels go off the floor, and return the upper body to center and the arms to neutral as in count 1.

4   Straighten the knees.

Repeat three times.

Note: On count 2, be sure the armswing and the straightening of the knees are done simultaneously.

Do this exercise in second position parallel.

plié EXERCISE 4

Stand in first position parallel, but instead of keeping the arms neutral, lift them forward until they are parallel to the floor, with the palms toward the floor. (This exercise should *not* be performed by beginners until they have learned to hold the body weight so that no strain is put on the ligaments that attach to the knees.)

Count 1 Plié in an easy bounce toward the floor so that the heels leave the floor slightly.

2 Continue the plié with the bounce, going closer to the floor so that the heels go higher.

3 Bounce-plié still closer to the floor.

4 Continue to bounce-plié to end by holding a sitting position close to the floor. The weight should be supported on the balls of the feet, and the arms should remain parallel to the floor, with the palms toward the floor.

Count 1 Bounce-plié, moving slightly away from the floor.

2 Bounce-plié, moving farther from the floor so that the heels lower.

3 Bounce-plié, moving still farther from the floor so that the heels almost touch the floor.

4 Bounce-plié to end in a standing position with the knees straight and the heels on the floor.

Repeat three times.

Note: The bounce-pliés should be done very smoothly.

Count 1-4 Plié to a sitting position, with the heels off the floor.

Count 5-8 Straighten the knees and lower the heels to return to a standing position.

'Repeat three times.

Note: All eight counts should be performed smoothly, in one continuous movement with no break.

fEET aNd lEq ExERCiSE 1

Stand in regular first position — with the feet turned out. Keeping the elbows straight, lift the arms diagonally up, with the palms toward the floor.

Count 1   Bend the right knee, lift the right heel, and push through the arch, lifting the heel farther from the floor.

2   Push farther through the arch so that only the tip of the toe touches the floor.

3   Lower the front part of the foot so that it returns to the position at the end of count 1.

4   Lower the heel to the floor and straighten the knee.

Repeat with the left foot.

Repeat on both sides at least three times.

fEET aNd lEq ExERCiSE 2

Stand in regular first position and lift the arms diagonally up, with the palms toward the floor, as in the preceding exercise.

Count 1   Brush the right foot diagonally forward, keeping the knee straight. Brush through to a point.

2   Pull the right leg back to place, leading with the heel.

3-4   Repeat counts 1 and 2 on the left side.

Note: The body weight should stay centered over the supporting leg.

Count 1   Brush the right foot diagonally forward six to eight inches off the floor, to a point.

2   Pull the leg back to place. Allow the foot to remain pointed until the ball of the foot touches the floor. Then the heel leads in pulling the leg back to place.

3-4   Repeat counts 1 and 2 on the left side.

Count 1   Brush the right foot diagonally forward off the floor to waist height.

2   Pull the leg back to place. Allow the foot to remain pointed until the ball of the foot touches the floor. Then the heel leads in pulling the leg back to place.

3-4   Repeat counts 1 and 2 on the left side.

Do these brushes on both sides at all three levels—on the floor, six to eight inches off the floor, and at waist height—twice as slowly. That is, use two counts for each movement instead of one.

Lunge stretch 1

Stand in first position parallel—that is, with the feet parallel but not quite touching—but instead of keeping the arms neutral, lift them directly to the sides until they are in second position.

Count 1   Step-lunge directly forward as far as possible with the right leg, keeping the right foot on the floor, bending the right knee, and moving the arms straight forward—parallel to the floor and with the palms toward the floor. The left heel leaves the floor slightly but the left knee remains straight. The torso should form a diagonal line from the head to the hip.

and   Straighten the right knee.

2   Bend the right knee.

and   Straighten the right knee.

3   Bend the right knee.

and   Straighten the right knee.

4   Bend the right knee.

and   Swing the left leg forward through first position while straightening the right knee, and then return the left foot to the floor in first position parallel. During the leg motion, return the arms directly to second position.

Repeat on the left side.

Repeat again on both sides.

Lunge Stretch 2

Stand in first position parallel, this time keeping the arms neutral (hanging relaxed at the sides).

Count 1   Step-lunge directly forward with the right leg, placing the entire foot on the floor and bending the right knee in a plié. Lift the arms straight forward until they are parallel to the floor, with the palms toward the floor.

    2   Take a deeper plié in the right knee.

    3   Take a still deeper plié in the right knee. Take the plié as far as possible without letting the right foot leave the floor. The right foot should remain on the floor after the plié as well as during the movement.

    4   Straighten the right knee and move both hands to hold the lower right leg. At the same time, round the back to bring the head as close to the right knee as possible.

  and   Plié slightly in the right knee. Then swing the left leg straight forward off the floor to stand in first position parallel, and at the same time return the arms to neutral.

Repeat once more on the same side.

Repeat two times on the left side.

Lunge Stretch 3

Stand in first position parallel.

Count 1   Step-lunge directly forward with the right foot, sitting deep enough in a plié in the right knee so that the right heel does not touch the floor. At the same time, lift the arms straight forward parallel to the floor, with the palms toward the floor. The left leg should be as straight as possible, and each hip should be about eight inches from the floor. (The distance between the hip and the floor will vary depending on body structure and flexibility; the important consideration is to stretch through the legs, forward and back, as far as possible.)

and   Bounce easily in the lunge, pulling slightly away from the floor.

2   Bounce slightly toward the floor.

and   Bounce slightly away from the floor.

3   Bounce slightly toward the floor.

and   Bounce away from the floor.

4   Straighten the right knee and move both hands to hold the lower right leg. At the same time, round the back to bring the head as close to the right knee as possible. (The left leg remains in place.)

and   Bounce slightly toward the floor. Then swing the left leg straight forward off the floor to stand in first position parallel, and at the same time return the arms to neutral.

Repeat once more on the same side, but this time stop at the end of count 4 so that the right knee is straight, both hands grasp the lower right leg, the back is rounded, and the head is as close to the right knee as possible.

Two-Count Changeover to the Left Side

Count 1   Straighten the back, lift the head, and bring the arms forward until they are parallel to the floor with the palms toward the floor.

and   Lift the ball of the left foot slightly off the floor and begin to bring the left leg forward.

2   Continue to bring the left leg forward, keeping the body weight forward. Place the left foot next to the right foot and lower the arms to neutral to stand in first position parallel.

Repeat the lunge stretch two times on the left side.

Combination Stretch 1

Count 1   2

Lunge stretch 4

Stand in first position parallel.

Count 1   Step-lunge *deep* directly forward with the right foot so that the hip is close to the floor. At the same time, lift the arms straight forward parallel to the floor, with the palms toward the floor. The left leg should be as straight as possible.

      and   Bounce easily away from the floor.

      2   Bounce easily toward the floor.

      and   Bounce easily away from the floor.

      3   Bounce easily toward the floor.

      and   Bounce easily away from the floor.

      4   Bring the left leg forward to pass the right and place the entire foot on the floor. Then plié, allowing the left heel to lift.

Combination stretch 1

Stand in regular second position — that is, with the feet turned out and twelve to twenty-four inches apart, with the arms lifted to the sides, and with the palms toward the floor. However, instead of holding the arms directly to the sides, hold them diagonally forward, keeping the elbows straight.

Count 1   Push through the arch of the right foot, lifting the heel and bending the knee. Reach upward through the right arm and lower the left shoulder, bending the left elbow. (See the illustration.)

      and   Lower the right heel.

      2   Push through the arch of the left foot, lifting the heel and bending the knee. Reach upward through the left arm and lower the right shoulder, bending the right elbow. (See the illustration.)

and   Lower the left heel.

3   Push through the arch of the right foot and repeat the other actions of count 1.

and   Lower the right heel.

4   Push through the arch of the left foot and repeat the other actions of count 2.

and   Lower the left heel.

5-8   Repeat counts 1 through 4.

Repeat all eight counts three times.

Note: The hip is always extended on the side opposite the bent knee and the lifted arm.

COMbiNATiON STRETCH 2

Stand in regular second position but with the arms diagonally forward, as at the beginning of the first combination stretch, described above.

Count 1   Repeat the action of count 1 above. In addition, begin to round the back so that the head moves forward, toward the left knee (the straight one).

and   Lower the right heel and continue to round the back and move the head forward.

2   Repeat the action of count 2 above, and in addition continue to round the back so that the head moves forward, toward the right knee now (the straight one).

and   Lower the left heel and continue to round the back and move the head forward.

3-8   Repeat counts 3 through 8 above, and in addition continue to round the back so that the head moves forward, toward the knees.

Count 1-8 Repeat the action of counts 1 through 8 of the first combination stretch, but this time gradually straighten the back and lift the head to return to the starting position.

Extension 1

Pressed position

Note: The rounding of the back and the movement of the head forward should take a full eight counts, and the straightening and lifting should also take eight counts.

Do this combination stretch with a rounding of the back diagonally to the right and a return, and then a rounding diagonally to the left and a return. Then do the combination with a rounding straight forward in only four counts instead of eight, and a return in four counts.

EXTENSION 1

Stand in first position parallel, but with the arms and hands in "pressed position." To reach the pressed position, hold the arms directly to the sides and bend the elbows to bring the wrists toward the rib cage until they are less than two inches away from the rib cage. Hold the palms toward the front, extend the fingers and move them apart, and press the heels of the hands forward. (See the illustration.)

Count 1   Lift the right leg forward with the knee bent until the thigh is parallel to the floor. The left knee remains straight.

2   Extend the lower right leg directly forward from the knee and flex the right foot.

3   Bring the right leg back to the position at the end of count 1.

4   Bring the right foot to the floor, to return to the starting position.

Repeat on the left side.

Count 1   Lift the right leg forward with the knee bent until the thigh is parallel to the floor.

2   Extend the lower right leg directly *backward* from the knee and flex the right foot.

3   Bring the right leg back to the position at the end of count 1.

4   Bring the right leg to the floor to return to the starting position.

Repeat on the left side.

Count 1   Lift the right leg forward with the knee bent until the thigh is parallel to the floor.

2   Extend the right leg sideward to the right and flex the right foot.

3   Bring the right leg back to the position at the end of count 1.

4   Bring the right leg to the floor to return to the starting position.

Repeat on the left side.

Repeat the extension exercise on both sides in all three directions: forward, backward, and sideward.

EXTENSION 2

Stand in first position parallel, but with the arms and hands in pressed position, as for the previous extension exercise.

Count 1   Lift the right leg forward with the knee bent until the thigh is parallel to the floor. Plié in the left knee.

2   Extend the lower right leg directly forward from the knee and flex the right foot. Straighten the left knee.

3   Bring the right leg back to the position at the end of count 1. Plié in the left knee.

4   Straighten the right knee and at the same time bring the right foot to the floor to return to the starting position. Straighten the left knee.

Repeat on the left side.

Count 1   Lift the right leg forward with the knee bent until the thigh is parallel to the floor. Plié in the left knee.

2   Extend the lower right leg directly *backward* from the knee and flex the right foot. Straighten the left knee.

3   Bring the right leg back to the position at the end of count 1. Plié in the left knee.

4   Straighten the right knee and at the same time bring the right foot to the floor to return to the starting position. Straighten the left knee.

Repeat on the left side.

Count 1   Lift the right leg forward with the knee bent until the thigh is parallel to the floor. Plié in the left knee.

2   Extend the right leg sideward to the right and flex the right foot. Straighten the left knee.

3   Bring the right leg back to the position at the end of count 1. Plié in the left knee.

4   Straighten the right knee and at the same time bring the right foot to the floor to return to the starting position. Straighten the left knee.

Repeat on the left side.

Repeat this extension exercise on both sides in all three directions: forward, backward, and sideward.

Note: On each count 1, start the lifting of the leg and the plié at the same time.

Do the entire extension exercise twice as slowly, taking two counts to move to each position. (Thus, count 1 becomes counts 1 and 2; count 2 becomes counts 3 and 4; etc.) Advanced students may do the exercise in three counts for each position. (Thus, count 1 becomes counts 1, 2, and 3; count 2 becomes counts 4, 5, and 6; etc.) The more counts used to move to a position, the more advanced the students need to be.

CONTRACTION EXERCISE 1

Because contractions are essential to jazz dance, it is extremely important that students develop the movement well. Beginning students may gain the feeling of the movement by starting in a position lying on the back with the arms in neutral position – that is, relaxed at the sides. Normally there is a small space between the lower back and the floor. In the movement, abdominal muscles should pull the lower back to the floor (in some cases, the knees must bend to accomplish this).

Count 1   Contract the lower back to the floor.

    and   Release the contraction and relax.

    Repeat three times.

Count 1   Contract the lower back to the floor.

    and   Hold the position.

    2   Release and relax.

    Repeat three times.

Note: The exercise should begin with a slow tempo and, as familiarity with the movement increases, the tempo should become quicker.

CONTRACTION EXERCISE 2

Beginning students may gain the feeling of the contraction while standing by imagining that a string is going through the center of the waist and that someone behind is pulling the string very slowly and then releasing it to allow the waist and hips to move back to place. The imaginary string may be pulled quickly and released slowly or vice versa. Once the sense of the center contraction is developed, it can be transferred to other parts of the body.

Stand in a slightly open first position parallel with the arms neutral.

Count 1   Begin to contract the center of the body. The knees will begin to bend.

    2   Continue the contraction. The heels will begin to leave the floor.

    3   Continue the contraction.

    4   Complete the contraction so that the body is hollow and there is a straight vertical line from the shoulder to the bent knee.

Count 1   Begin to release the contraction. The knees and the center of the body will begin to straighten.

    2   Continue the release.

    3   Continue the release.

4   Complete the release so that the body is back in the starting position.

Repeat the contraction and the release three times.

Note: Both the contraction and the release should be done as one smooth, continuous movement.

Count 1   Begin to contract as in the preceding counts, and at the same time begin to rotate the arms toward the center of the body, with the elbows slightly rounded.

2   Continue the contraction and the rotation of the arms. At the same time, begin to lift the arms forward and upward.

3   Continue the contraction and the rotation and lifting of the arms.

4   Complete the movement so that the arms are about a foot from the knees.

Count 1-4   Release the contraction and return the arms to neutral.

Repeat the contraction and the release three times.

Do the contraction and the release without the arm movement, but use only two counts instead of four, and repeat this three times. Then do the exercise with the arm movement in two counts and repeat this three times.

CONTRACTION EXERCISE 3

Stand in a slightly open first position parallel with the arms neutral.

Count 1   Contract sharply in the center and at the same time rotate the arms and elbows forward.

and   Contract sharply again. At the same time, bring the arms farther forward.

a   Contract sharply again. Bring the arms still farther forward.

2   Finish the contraction sharply to the deepest point possible (the heels *may* leave the floor), and bring the arms as far forward as possible.

3-4   Release the body and arms back to the starting position in one smooth, continuous movement.

Repeat three times.

Note: In the first two counts, the arms and body should work together in sharp spurts of movement that contrast with the smooth release.

CONTRACTION EXERCISE 4

Stand in a slightly open first position parallel with the arms neutral.

Count 1   Contract sharply in the center and at the same time rotate the arms and elbows forward.

and   Contract sharply again. At the same time, bring the arms farther forward.

a   Contract sharply again. Bring the arms still farther forward.

2   Finish the contraction sharply to the deepest point possible, with a straight line from the shoulder to the knee, and bring the arms still farther forward.

3   Release the body sharply and at the same time reverse the movement of the arms.

a   Continue the release of the body and the return of the arms, keeping a sharp quality.

4   Complete the release and the return so that the arms and the center of the body are back in the starting position.

Repeat three times.

CONTRACTION EXERCISE 5

This exercise and the two that follow offer varying uses of smooth, flowing movement and sharp, strong spurts of movement. Move the arms at the same time and with the same quality as the center of the body, and take each contraction as far as possible with the heels remaining on the floor.

Stand in a slightly open first position parallel with the arms neutral.

Count 1 Contract sharply.

  and Continue smoothly.

  a Continue smoothly.

  2 Continue smoothly.

  3 Continue sharply.

  and Continue sharply.

  4 Finish the contraction sharply.

  5-8 Release in one smooth, continuous movement.

  Repeat three times.

Count 1-8 Reverse the preceding movement: do a smooth contraction for four counts and then a rhythmic release — sharp, smooth, sharp — like the contraction of the preceding movement.

  Repeat three times.

CONTRACTION EXERCISE 6

Stand in a slightly open first position with the arms neutral.

Count 1 Contract smoothly.

  and Continue smoothly.

  a Continue sharply.

  2 Continue sharply.

  and Continue sharply.

  a Continue sharply.

  3 Continue sharply.

  and Continue sharply.

  a Continue smoothly.

  4 Continue smoothly.

  and Finish the contraction smoothly.

5-8   Release in one smooth continuous movement.

Repeat three times.

Count 1-8   Reverse the preceding movement: do a smooth contraction and a rhythmic release.

Repeat three times.

CONTRACTION EXERCISE 7

Stand in a slightly open first position with the arms neutral.

Count 1   Contract smoothly.

and   Continue sharply.

a   Continue sharply.

3   Continue sharply.

and   Continue sharply.

a   Continue sharply.

4   Finish the contraction sharply.

5-8   Release in one smooth, continuous movement.

Repeat three times.

Count 1-8   Reverse the preceding movement: do a smooth contraction and a rhythmic release.

Repeat three times.

Note: Besides the many variations of smooth and sharp movement possible in four counts, there are variations of the count itself. For example, contraction exercises 5, 6, and 7 can each be adapted to basic counts of six, eight, ten, or twelve.

CONTRACTION EXERCISE 8

(Full Contraction)

During this contraction, the body moves to a position in which the knees (in plié) are not more than a foot and a half from the floor, and there is a straight line from the shoulder to the knee. The heels lift

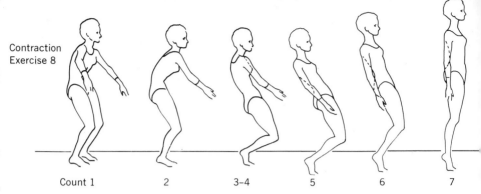

Contraction
Exercise 8

Count 1   2   3–4   5   6   7

gradually from the floor as the contraction continues. (See the illustrations.) This contraction is quite demanding on the thighs, and it should *not* be done by beginners. Nor should it be done by any class until the students are thoroughly warmed up.

Stand in second position parallel – that is, with the feet parallel and twelve to twenty-four inches apart – but with the arms neutral (hanging relaxed at the sides).

Count 1	Contract in the center, allowing the knees to bend, the arms to rotate forward (so that the palms turn toward the front), and the heels to leave the floor.
2	Continue the contraction and the forward rotation of the arms.
3	Continue the contraction and the forward rotation of the arms.
4	Finish the contraction to the deepest point possible, so that the plié is as deep as possible, with the body balancing on the balls of the feet, and the arms almost parallel to the floor.
5	Begin to straighten the knees and to reverse the movement of the arms so that the palms turn toward the sides as the arms rotate.
6	Continue the release and the movement of the arms.
7	Continue the release and the movement of the arms until the body is centered and the arms are neutral, though the heels are off the floor.
8	Lower the heels to the floor.

Repeat the contraction and the release three times.

CONTRACTION EXERCISE 9

Repeat the full contraction with the addition of the rhythmic variations (done in four basic counts) of contraction exercises 5, 6, and 7. Adapt these variations to basic counts of six, eight, ten, and twelve as well.

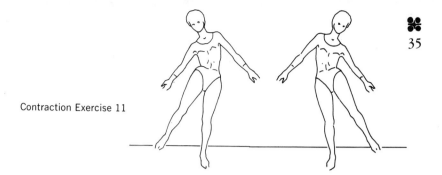

Contraction Exercise 11

CONTRACTION EXERCISE 10

Repeat the full contraction but hold for four counts before the release. That is, contract in four counts, hold for four counts, and release in four counts. Intermediate and advanced students may contract in six counts, hold for six counts, and release in six counts; and contract in ten counts, hold for ten counts, and release in ten.

CONTRACTION EXERCISE 11

(Side Contraction)

Besides the usual forward contractions in the center of the body, there are contractions done on either side of the center. It is important to distinguish between a right or left hip lift and a right or left side contraction. A hip lift is done by simply lifting the hip, and usually the foot on the same side leaves the floor slightly. A side contraction, however, is done by contracting the muscles between the waist and the hip, thereby *causing* the hip to be lifted.

Stand in second position parallel — that is, with the feet parallel and twelve to twenty-four inches apart — but with the arms neutral (hanging relaxed at the sides).

Count 1-4	Contract the right side smoothly. (See the illustration.)
1-4	Release smoothly.
1-4	Contract the left side smoothly. (See the illustration.)
1-4	Release smoothly.
Count 1	Contract the right side sharply.
2	Release smoothly.
Count 1	Contract the left side sharply.
2	Release smoothly.
Count 1	Contract the right side sharply.
2	Release sharply.
Count 1	Contract the left side sharply.
2	Release sharply.

Count 1 Contract the right side sharply.

 and Release sharply.

 2 Contract the left side sharply.

 and Release sharply.

Repeat the last set of counts ("1 and 2 and") for eight consecutive counts, relax for a moment, and repeat the eight counts.

CONTRACTION EXERCISE 12

(Combination Front and Side Contraction)

Stand in second position parallel with the arms neutral.

Count 1 Contract in the center so that the hip area is brought forward.

 and Release the hips to center.

 2 Contract the right side.

 and Release the hips to center.

 3 Contract the left side.

 and Release the hips to center.

Repeat at least three times.

Note: Between the contractions, always bring the hip area back to center.

Do the exercise in varying directions: after contracting forward, side right, and side left, contract forward, side left, and side right.

Do the exercise with the variation of a sharp quality of movement.

Count 1 Contract in the center so that the hip area is brought forward, and let the right foot leave the floor no more than a few inches.

 and Release the hips to center and allow the foot to move back to place.

 2 Contract the right side and allow the right foot to leave the floor.

and Release the hips to center and allow the foot to move back to place.

3 Contract the left side and allow the left foot to leave the floor.

and Release the hips to center and allow the foot to move back to place.

Repeat at least two times.

Do these four counts but let the *left* foot leave the floor on count 1.

Do the four counts in varying directions: after contracting forward, side right, and side left, contract forward, side left, and side right, with matching foot movement.

body Roll 1

The body roll develops fluidity, control, and the ability to articulate the back and parts of the back. A complete body roll is a total movement that is described fully in the following exercises. This first body roll is a beginning exercise, done above the waist only: the chest moves forward and upward and then describes a half circle downward and another half circle to return, with the head following. The movement is done by muscular control of the back and head, not by collapsing them.

Stand in second position parallel—that is, with the feet parallel and twelve to twenty-four inches apart—but place the heels of the hands against the tops of the thighs on either side. Hold the fingers in a slant diagonally downward, and bend the elbows out to the sides. Keep the legs and knees in place throughout this exercise.

Count 1 Begin to lift the chest upward and forward and at the same time let the chin begin to lift upward and forward.

2 Continue the lift and forward movement of the chest and the lift of the chin.

3 Move the chest forward and downward so that the back becomes parallel to the floor, with the head following slightly above the back.

Body Roll 2

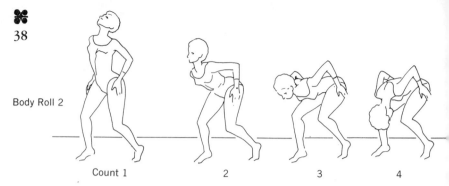

Count 1   2   3   4

4 Continue the movement so that the back is diagonal to the floor, with the head following.

and Finish the movement of the head so that it catches up to the back, moving into the same line as the back.

5 Begin to lift the lowest section of the back to center, letting the rest of the back and the head remain forward.

6 Lift a higher section of the back to center, causing the head to move closer to the chest.

7 Continue to lift the back to center until only the head is forward.

8 Lift the head to center.

Repeat three times.

Note: The entire eight counts should be done as one continuous movement, with no breaks.

body roll 2

(Complete Body Roll)

Stand in second position parallel, as in the preceding exercise, but place the right foot a few inches forward. Hold the hands and arms as in the preceding exercise. (See the illustrations.)

Count 1-4 Repeat the upper body movement of counts 1 through 4 of the preceding exercise, and also plié. The plié should be deepest in the left knee at the end of count 4.

5-8 Lift the back and head to center as in the preceding exercise, and also straighten the knees. The knees should return to the starting position (with the right knee straight and the left knee in a slight plié) at the end of count 8.

Repeat three times.

Do the body roll down with a plié in two counts instead of four, and lift the back and head while straightening the knees in two counts. Repeat three times.

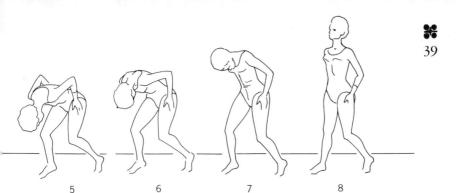

5 6 7 8

Do the body roll down with a plié in one count, and return in one count. Repeat three times.

Do the complete body roll in four counts, then two counts, and then one count with the *left* foot a few inches forward, and repeat each time (count) variation three times.

body roll 3.

Stand as in Body Roll 2 (with the legs in second position parallel but the right foot a few inches forward, with the heels of the hands against the tops of the thighs and the fingers slanted diagonally downward, and with the elbows bent out to the sides). Pull up to half toe.

Count 1-4   Starting from half toe, do the plié and the forward roll of the preceding exercise.

Count 5-8   Repeat counts 5 through 8 of the preceding exercise. At the end of count 8, pull up to half toe.

Repeat three times.

Do the body roll on half toe with the *left* foot a few inches forward, and repeat three times.

body roll 4

(Three-Direction Roll)

Stand as in Body Roll 1, so that the right foot is *not* forward.

Count 1-4   Plié while doing the forward roll.

Count 5-8   Straighten the knees as the back and head are lifted to center.

and   Turn the body to face diagonally right (this means that the right foot will be slightly forward and the left foot will have the heel off the floor, where it will stay until the weight is shifted when the body is turned to center again).

Count 1-4	Plié while doing the forward roll.
Count 5-8	Straighten the knees as the back and head are lifted to center.
and	Turn to center, shifting the weight to both feet evenly and standing as at the beginning of the exercise.
Count 1-4	Plié while doing the forward roll.
Count 5-8	Straighten the knees as the back and head are lifted to center.
and	Turn the body to face diagonally left, so that the left foot is slightly forward and the heel of the right foot is off the floor.
Count 1-4	Plié while doing the forward roll.
Count 5-8	Straighten the knees as the back and head are lifted to center.
and	Turn to center.

Do the full sequence of directions (center, right, center, left) in four counts instead of eight for each direction.

Do the sequence in two counts (one for the plié and forward roll and one for the return) for each direction.

Do the sequence in one count for each direction.

body Roll 5

(Reverse Body Roll)

Stand as in Body Roll 1 (with the legs and feet in second position parallel, with the heels of the hands against the tops of the thighs and the fingers diagonally downward, and with the elbows bent out to the sides).

Count 1	Pull the chest directly backward and let the head begin to drop slightly forward.
2	Continue the dropping of the chest backward, toward the floor, while the head drops forward.

3   Lift the chest forward and upward, and let the head begin to move upward.

4   Complete the movement of the chest and head so that they return to center.

Repeat three times.

Do the reverse body roll in two counts instead of four. Repeat. Then do the reverse body roll in one count and repeat.

Do the reverse body roll with a plié in four counts. Repeat. Then do the body roll with a plié in two counts and in one count, repeating each.

Do the reverse body roll with a plié in four counts and pull up to half toe at the end of count four. Repeat. Then do the body roll and plié ending on half toe in two counts and in one count, repeating each.

body roll 6

(Complete Reverse Body Roll)

Stand in second position parallel with the arms neutral (hanging relaxed at the sides).

Count 1   Bend backward from the waist to achieve a position in which the back is flat. Keep the head in line with the back, as though the head were an extension of the spine. At the same time, move the arms forward until they are parallel to the floor and held close to the hips.

2   Plié without dropping the hips; there should be a straight line from the hip to the head.

3   Push the hips forward to lead the upper body toward center. At the end of the count there should be a straight (diagonal) line from the knee to the head.

4   Continue to bring the upper body to center as the knees are straightened.

Note: It is very important not to drop the hips on count 3. In a sense, the hips replace the head in keying the movement.

body ROLL 7

(Reverse Body Roll from a Sitting Position)

Sit on the floor with the legs in first position parallel – that is, with the feet parallel but not quite touching – and point the toes. Hold the arms in second position (to the sides) and turn the palms forward.

Count 1   Begin to lower the back to the floor. At the same time, let the head drop forward and the arms begin to close.

2   Continue to lower the back to the floor, and let the head drop farther forward while the arms continue to close.

3   Continue to lower the back to the floor and to move the arms closer to the sides.

4   Let the head touch the floor last. By this time, the entire back is on the floor and the arms are in first position parallel, quite close to the sides with the palms toward the sides.

5   Place the arms next to the sides and turn the palms so that the fingertips press the floor for support. Begin to lift the lower back away from the floor.

6   Continue the lifting (arching) of the back, with the head following.

7   Continue the lifting through the chest, with the head following.

8   Complete the movement of the back and head to center, and at the same time return the arms to their starting position.

Repeat.

Note: Beginners may find it helpful to press the lower back to the floor at the start of the lift in count 5, so that the sitting up is an exact reverse of the earlier counts.

3

rhythmic exercises and sequences

Students of jazz dance must develop a good sense of timing. As a start, they must be able to distinguish the beat from the afterbeat as readily as right from left. It is easy to hear the basic beat in some music, but not so easy in the complex rhythmic structure of other music. I suggest that a variety of selections of varying complexity be used, especially in the basic exercises in this chapter (see the records listed in the chapter on music).

This chapter, like the others, progresses from simple to difficult exercises. One important aim of the progression is to aid the students in developing their rhythmic sense.

CENTER floor exercise 1

Stand in an easy (relaxed) first position parallel—that is, with the feet parallel but not quite touching and the arms neutral (hanging relaxed at the sides). Face to the front and move to the right.

Count 1   Step to the right side about six inches with the right foot. (Keep the arms neutral.)

and   Bend the right knee.

2   Step to the right side with the left foot, crossing the right foot. Immediately following, lift the right foot off the floor.

and   Bend the left knee.

3-8   Continue stepping to the right side in this order. On the "and" following count 8, bend the left knee and immediately change direction to move to the left.

Count 1   Step to the left side with the right foot, crossing the left foot and allowing the body to face diagonally to the left a little. (The direction of movement is the reverse of the first eight counts.)

and   Bend the right knee.

2   Step to the left side about six inches with the left foot.

and   Bend the left knee.

3-8   Continue in this order. On the "and" following count 8, bend the left knee and prepare to move forward.

Count 1   Step directly forward with the right foot.

and   Bend the right knee.

2   Step directly forward with the left foot.

and   Bend the left knee.

3-8   Continue to step directly forward in this order. On the "and" following count 8, bend the left knee and prepare to move backward.

Count 1   Step directly backward with the right foot.

and   Bend the right knee.

2   Step directly forward with the left knee.

and   Bend the left knee.

3-8   Continue in this order. On the "and" following count 8, bend the left knee.

Do this exercise only up to the "and" following count 7 for each direction. (In seven or any other odd number of counts, the exercise begins to the right with the right foot, starts to the left with the left foot, moves forward beginning with the right foot, and moves backward beginning with the left foot. In even counts, each direction begins with the right foot. In any number of counts, the final "and" is completed on the left foot with a bending of the left knee.)

Do the exercise only up to the "and" following count 6 for each direction. Then do the exercise only up to the "and" following count 5 in each direction, then 4, 3, 2, and 1.

CENTER floor EXERCiSE 2

Stand in an easy first position parallel, as in the preceding exercise.

Count 1   Step to the right side about six inches with the right foot, and at the same time focus the entire body to the right to face right.

    and   Bend the right knee.

    2   Step with the left foot to move in the same direction as in count 1.

    and   Bend the left knee.

    3-8   Continue to step to the right while facing right. On the "and" following count 8, bend the left knee and immediately change direction to move to the left.

Count 1   Step to the left with the right foot, crossing the left foot, and at the same time focus the entire body to the left to face left. (The direction of movement is the reverse of the first eight counts.)

    and   Bend the right knee.

    2   Step with the left foot to continue moving to the left.

    and   Bend the left knee.

    3-8   Continue to step to the left while facing left. On the "and" following count 8, bend the left knee and prepare to move forward.

Count 1-8   Step directly forward, starting with the right foot, and on the "and" following count 8, bend the left knee and immediately change direction to move backward.

Count 1-8   Turning to face backward, step with the right foot and continue in the same direction. On the "and" following count 8, bend the left knee.

Do this exercise by using successively fewer counts in each direction. That is, do only up to the "and" following count 7 in each direction, then to 6, 5, 4, etc.

CENTER floor EXERCiSE 3

When the two preceding exercises are familiar, add a clap or finger snap on the afterbeat — at the same time as the plié. Then add two claps, one on the "and" count and the other on the "a" following.

CENTER floor EXERCiSE 4

Perform the breakdown from eight counts of Center Floor Exercise 1 twice as fast — in double time.

Do the breakdown with two groups of dancers. Both groups start together. One goes through the breakdown once in normal time while the other goes through the breakdown twice in double time. The groups should finish together. Reverse the groups and repeat.

CENTER floor EXERCiSE 5

Stand in an easy first position parallel — with the feet parallel but not quite touching and the arms neutral — as in Center Floor Exercise 1.

Count 1	Step diagonally forward and right a few inches with the right foot.
and	Cross the left foot in back of the right.
2	Again step diagonally forward and right a few inches with the right foot.
3	Step directly forward a few inches with the left foot.
4	Step with the right foot to bring it to place next to the left foot, with the weight on the ball of the right foot.
5-8	Hold this position, snapping the fingers or clapping the hands on the counts.

Repeat to the left, forward, and back, taking eight counts for each direction.

Count 1-4   Repeat the steps to the right described above.

5-7   Hold this position, snapping the fingers or clapping the hands on these three counts.

Repeat in the other three directions, taking seven counts for each direction.

Count 1-4   Repeat as above.

5-6   Hold this position, snapping the fingers or clapping the hands on these two counts.

Repeat in the other three directions, taking six counts for each direction.

Count 1-4   Repeat as above.

5   Hold this position and snap or clap on the count.

Repeat in the other three directions, taking five counts for each direction.

Count 1   Step diagonally forward and right a few inches with the right foot.

and   Cross the left foot in back of the right.

2   Again step diagonally forward and right a few inches with the right foot. Place the weight on the ball of the right foot.

3-4   Hold this position, snapping the fingers or clapping the hands on these two counts.

Repeat in the other three directions, taking four counts for each direction.

Count 1-2   Repeat the steps to the right described above.

3   Hold this position and snap or clap on the count.

Repeat in the other three directions, taking three counts for each direction.

Count 1-2   Repeat as above.

Repeat in the other three directions, taking two counts for each direction.

Count 1   Step to the right with the right foot.

Repeat in the other directions (step to the left with the left foot, forward with the right foot, and backward with the left foot). On the last step (backward with the left foot), snap the fingers or clap the hands.

Do this breakdown with two groups of dancers. Both groups start together. One goes through the breakdown once in normal time while the other goes through the breakdown twice in double time. The groups should finish together. Reverse the groups and repeat.

plié EXERCISE 1

Stand in first position parallel — with the feet parallel but not quite touching and the arms neutral (hanging relaxed at the sides).

Count 1   Continue to stand in first position parallel.

and   Bend both knees.

2   Straighten both knees.

and   Bend both knees.

Repeat.

Note: In bending, be sure each knee is directed over the center of the foot.

plié EXERCISE 2

Stand in first position parallel.

Count 1   Remaining in place, step on the right foot so that the whole foot touches the floor.

and   Bend the right knee and lift the left foot off the floor.

2   Step on the left foot so that the whole foot touches the floor.

and   Bend the left knee and lift the right foot off the floor.

Repeat.

Do the exercise in four counts, stepping forward rather than remaining

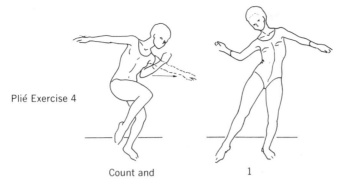

Plié Exercise 4

Count and   1

in place, and then do four counts stepping backward. Start the forward and the backward steps with the right foot.

plié EXERCISE 3

Repeat Plié Exercise 1 once, then do Plié Exercise 2 twice, remaining in place, and finally do the forward-and-back variation of Plié Exercise 2 once.

plié EXERCISE 4

Stand in first position parallel, with the feet easy (comfortably apart and open rather than carefully positioned) and with the arms in second position (extended directly to the sides).

Count and   Plié in the left knee and bring the right knee diagonally across the left thigh. At the same time bend the left elbow and bring it in toward the center of the body. This causes the upper body to tilt slightly to the left. (See the illustration.)

1   Stretch the right leg directly to the right side with the toe toward the floor, and straighten the left knee slightly. At the same time return the left arm to second position and bend the right elbow down a little, rotating the hand so that the palm is forward, as the upper body tilts slightly to the right. (See the illustration.)

and   Repeat the movements of the first "and" count, starting from the position at the end of count 1. (Return the right arm to second position as a part of the movement.)

2   Repeat count 1.

and   Repeat the first "and" count, returning the right arm to second position as a part of the movement.

3-4   Continue to repeat the movements.

Repeat all four counts on the other side, starting with a plié in the right knee and a bending of the right elbow.

plié EXERCISE 5

Stand in first position parallel, with the feet easy (comfortably apart and open rather than carefully positioned) and the arms neutral (hanging relaxed at the sides).

Count and   Remaining in place, lift the right foot away from the floor and at the same time bend the left knee.

1   Step with the right foot so that the whole foot touches the floor and at the same time straighten the left knee.

and   Lift the left foot away from the floor and at the same time bend the right knee.

2   Step with the left foot so that the whole foot touches the floor and at the same time straighten the right knee.

Repeat.

plié EXERCISE 6

Repeat plié exercises 1, 2 (including the forward-and-back variation), and 5 in sequence.

When the sequence is performed well, add a clap to the "and" and the "a" after each count, so that the count is followed by two claps.

CATCH STEP EXERCISE 1

Stand in first position parallel — with the feet parallel but not quite touching and the arms neutral (hanging relaxed at the sides).

Count and   Step forward with the left foot. Immediately bend the right knee and lift it until the foot is about five inches off the floor, and begin to move the knee backward.

a   Continue to move the right leg backward.

1   Step with the right foot about eighteen inches behind the left foot, and immediately lift the left foot slightly off the floor.

2   Step in place with the left foot.

3   Step forward with the right foot.

4   Step forward with the left foot.

Repeat on the other side and then repeat on each side.

Note: The knees should remain in a plié throughout the exercise, and the plié should be deepest on count 1. On the counts "and" and "a" the knee should be lifted upward and backward in one continuous motion, like a cycling movement.

CATch STEP EXERCISE 2

Stand in first position parallel. Repeat the steps of the previous exercise, starting by stepping with the left foot and lifting the right knee, and add the following arm movements.

Count and   Begin to bend the elbows and to turn the palms toward the ceiling, with the hands slightly cupped.

a   Continue to lift the arms, but no higher than waist level.

1   Turn the wrists over so that the palms are toward the floor, and push the heels of the hands toward the floor.

2   While stepping with the left foot, lift the right arm forward and parallel to the floor, and at the same time lift the left arm sideward until it is slightly below shoulder level.

3   While stepping with the right foot, reverse the position of the arms.

4   While stepping with the left foot, return the arms to the position of count 2.

Repeat, starting with the right foot, and reverse the movement of the arms on counts 2 and 3. Then repeat on each side.

When the arm movement is performed well, add a shoulder movement: Each time an arm is lifted forward, pull the same shoulder forward, and pull the other shoulder — the one over the sideward arm — to the back.

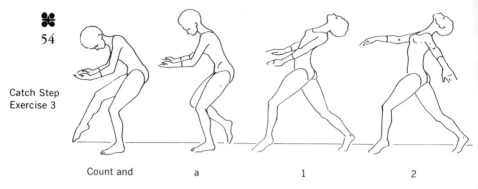

54

Catch Step
Exercise 3

| Count and | a | 1 | 2 |

CATCH STEP EXERCISE 3

(Complete Catch Step)

Stand in first position parallel. Repeat the steps and the arm movements of the previous exercises, starting by stepping with the left foot and lifting the right knee, and add the following body roll.

Count and   Begin to lower the head to the chest. (See the illustration.)

     a   Begin to lift the chest upward and diagonally forward and let the head begin to lift. (See the illustration.)

     1   Continue to lift the chest and the head diagonally upward. The head should now be focused so that there is a diagonal line extending from the chin to the ceiling. (See the illustration.)

   2-4   Continue to hold the position attained at the end of count 1. (See the illustrations.)

         Repeat on the other side and then repeat on each side.

Note: This body roll is not complete, but like a complete body roll it should be done as one smooth, continuous movement. When the steps begin with the right foot, the head should tilt so that the right ear is close to the right shoulder on count 1. When the steps begin with the left foot, the head should tilt slightly to the left side on count 1.

CATCH STEP EXERCISE 4

Stand in first position parallel.

Count 1-4   Repeat the steps and the arm, shoulder, and body-roll movements of the previous exercise (in other words, do a catch step), starting with the right foot.

     5   Step with the left foot and bend the knees.

   and   Clap the hands.

     6   Step with the right foot and bend the knees.

   and   Clap the hands.

     7   Step with the left foot and bend the knees.

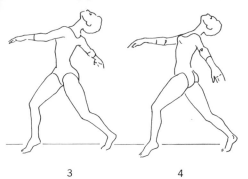

3   4

and   Clap the hands.

8   Step with the right foot.

Repeat, starting with the left foot.

CATCH STEP EXERCISE 5

Stand in first position parallel.

Count 1-4   Do a catch step, starting with the right foot.

5   Step with the left foot.

and   Bend the knees and clap.

a   Clap.

6   Step with the right foot.

and   Bend the knees and clap.

a   Clap.

7   Step with the left foot.

and   Bend the knees and clap.

a   Clap.

8   Step with the right foot.

Repeat, starting with the left foot.

CATCH STEP EXERCISE 6

Stand in first position parallel.

Count 1   Touch the right toe forward.

and   Step with the right foot.

2   Touch the left toe forward.

and   Step with the left foot.

3   Touch the right toe forward.

and   Step with the right foot.

4   Touch the left foot forward.

and   Step with the left foot.

a-5-8 Do a catch step, starting with the right foot.

Repeat, starting with the left foot.

Do the first four counts of this exercise and add counts 5 through 8 of Catch Step Exercise 5. Repeat, starting with the left foot.

CATCH STEP EXERCISE 7

Stand in first position parallel.

Count and- ⎫ Do the first part of a catch step, starting with the right
     a   ⎬ foot.

1   Step in place with the left foot, as in previous catch steps.

and   Instead of stepping forward with the right foot on count 2, bring the right to place next to the left foot on this count.

2-4   Bend the knees on each of these counts.

Repeat, starting on the left foot.

THREE—STEP EXERCISE 1

Stand in first position parallel — with the feet parallel but not quite touching and the arms neutral (hanging relaxed at the sides) — and plié in both knees. This exercise is done in place.

Count 1   Step with the right foot so that the whole foot touches the floor and the knee is in a deep plié.

2   Step with the ball of the left foot a few inches in back of the right foot, and straighten the left knee. (The right knee will straighten slightly at the same time and the right foot will almost leave the floor.)

3   Step with the right foot (the whole foot) in a deep plié.

Count 1   Step with the left foot (the whole foot) in a deep plié.

2   Step with the ball of the right foot a few inches in back of the left foot, and straighten the right knee. (Now the left

knee will straighten slightly and the left foot will almost
leave the floor.)

3   Step with the left foot (the whole foot) in a deep plié.

Repeat in place until the steps can be performed quite easily at
tempos varying from moderate to fast.

tHREE—STEP EXERCISE 2

Stand in first position parallel and plié in both knees. This exercise
moves across the floor.

Count 1   Take a long step forward and diagonally right with the
right foot, and plié deeply in the right knee. At the same
time, lift the left knee high.

2   Take a short step forward and diagonally right with the
left foot, and plié deeply in the left knee. At the same time,
lift the right knee high.

3   Take a short step forward and diagonally right with the
right foot, and plié deeply in the right knee. As in count
1, lift the left knee high.

Count 1-3   Repeat the three counts above, still moving diagonally
right, but start with the left foot.

Repeat all six counts above, but move diagonally left.

Note: By the lifting of one knee while the other is in a deep plié, this
exercise has a down-up-down quality. The exercise differs from Three-
Step Exercise 1 because the deep plié occurs on all counts, not just 1 and
3, and because the steps move in a long-short-short pattern rather than
remaining in place.

tHREE—STEP EXERCISE 3

Stand in first position parallel and hold the arms in second position—
extended in a long curve to the sides with the palms toward the floor.
Repeat the steps of the previous exercise, starting with the right foot,
and add the following arm movement.

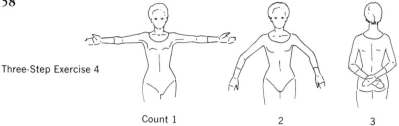

Three-Step Exercise 4

Count 1   2   3

Count 1 Move the right arm directly across the chest to end slightly in front of and lower than the left arm.

   2 Begin to move both arms downward and toward the right.

   3 Continue to move the arms until they are sideward right, the left slightly in front of and lower than the right.

  Repeat.

Note: The arms should go in one continuous motion and end almost absolutely straight, though the elbows remain slightly rounded.

tHREE—STEP EXERCiSE 4

Stand as in the preceding exercise. Repeat the steps of Three-Step Exercise 2, starting with the right foot, and add the following arm movement. (See the illustrations.)

Count 1 Straighten the elbows and turn the palms toward the front.

   2 Lower the arms and rotate them toward the body until the palms are toward the back. Bend the elbows during the lowering and rotation.

   3 Continue to lower the arms until they cross at the wrist.

  Repeat.

Note: Count 1 should be accented—done sharply—and counts 2 and 3 should be performed smoothly. There is a tendency to lift the shoulders on counts 2 and 3, and the shoulders should be pulled down with extra effort to counteract this tendency.

"STEP TOGETHER, STEP TOUCH" EXERCiSE 1

Stand in an easy (relaxed) first position parallel. The movement is forward on a series of diagonal lines, and all the steps are done in plié.

Count 1 Step diagonally right with the right foot so that the whole foot touches the floor.

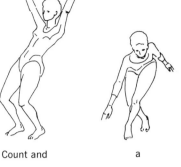

Shim Sham Variation 1

Count and   a

2   Lift the left foot and bring the ball of the foot to place next to the right.

3   Step diagonally left with the left foot so that the whole foot touches the floor.

4   Lift the right foot and bring the ball of the foot to place next to the left.

"step together, step touch" exercise 2

Stand in an easy first position parallel. Repeat the steps of the previous exercise twice (a total of eight counts), and add the following arm movement.

Count 1-4   Bend the arms at the elbows to move the forearms up from neutral position. Continue the movement so that the arms are upward and away from the body to cross at the wrists on count 4.

5-8   Open the arms slowly downward so that they reach second position—extended in a long curve to the sides with the palms toward the floor—at the end of count 8.

shim sham variation 1

Stand in first position parallel—with the feet parallel but not quite touching and the arms neutral (hanging relaxed at the sides).

Count and   Contract the hip directly forward, plié in both knees so that the body is leaning backward, and jump slightly off the floor to land in a deep plié with the right foot placed a little ahead of the left. At the same time, extend the arms upward in a "V" with the palms toward the front. (See the illustration.)

a   Shift the weight to the left foot and cross the right foot diagonally behind the left foot, stepping about six inches and touching the ball of the right foot against the floor.

Immediately release the hip and push it backward—
reversing the body line so that the upper body is leaning
forward—and at the same time bring the arms down. Move
the left arm to end at the left side with the hand about six
inches from the hip, and cross the right arm in front of the
body to end with the right hand about ten inches below
the left hand. (See the illustration.)

1   Step back to place with the right foot, shift the weight to
that foot, contract the hip directly forward, and plié in
both knees to lean backward as in the first "and" count. At
the same time, extend the arms upward in a "V" with the
palms toward the front.

and   Repeat the movement of the "a" count on the other side:
cross the left foot diagonally behind the right foot, stepping about six inches and touching the ball of the left foot
against the floor. Immediately release the hip and push it
backward—so that the upper body is leaning forward—
and at the same time bring the arms down so that the right
arm is at the right side with the hand about six inches from
the hip and the left arm is crossed in front of the body with
the hand about ten inches below the right hand.

2   Step back to place with the left foot, shift the weight to
that foot, contract the hip directly forward, and plié in
both knees to lean backward as before. At the same time,
extend the arms upward in a "V" with the palms toward
the front, also as before.

and   Cross the right foot diagonally behind the left foot and
repeat the other movement of the "a" count before count 1.

3   Repeat count 1.

and   Repeat the "and" count following count 1.

4   Repeat count 2.

Repeat all four counts on the other side: jump slightly and land
with the left foot forward, cross the left foot diagonally behind
the right foot on count "a," and so on.

shim sham variation 2

Stand with the feet in first position parallel, plié deeply in both knees, and crouch over with the head held up to look forward. Bend both elbows and hold the arms close to the rib cage.

Count and Moving slightly to the right, hop with the right foot.

1 Bring the left foot in next to the right and place the ball of the foot on the floor.

and Moving slightly to the left, hop with the left foot.

2 Bring the right foot in next to the left and place the ball of the foot on the floor.

and Moving diagonally backward and to the right, hop with the right foot.

3 Bring the left foot in next to the right and place the ball of the foot on the floor, as in count 1.

and Moving diagonally forward and to the left, hop with the left foot.

4 Bring the right foot in next to the left and place the ball of the foot on the floor, as in count 2.

Note: The body should stay in a crouched position throughout the steps and the arms should stay close to the rib cage. The upper body moves slightly from one side to the other, in opposition to the footwork.

shim sham variation 3

Stand as in the preceding exercise: place the feet in first position parallel, plié deeply in both knees, crouch over with the head held up to look forward, and hold the arms close to the rib cage with the elbows bent.

Count 1-4 Repeat the movement of the previous exercise.

5 Step straight forward with the right foot.

and Deepen the plié in both knees.

> 6   Step straight forward with the left foot.
>
> and   Deepen the plié in both knees.

Note: The upper body and the arms should maintain their positions, though the upper body moves slightly from one side to the other in opposition to the footwork, as in the previous exercise.

shim sham variation 4

Repeat the three preceding shim sham variations by starting Shim Sham Variation 1 with a jump with the right foot forward, then repeat Variation 1 starting with the left foot forward, then immediately go into Shim Sham Variation 2 and then into Variation 3.

Do the full sequence of movement with two groups of dancers. One group starts with Variation 1 on both sides and the other group starts at the same time with Variation 2, followed by Variation 3 and then Variation 1. This means that the first group will be emphasizing the first four beats while the second group accents the upbeats (the "and" counts before the beats). Once the students are able to work through the two patterns in two groups, they may mingle and try to repeat their own pattern. The students will need concentration because they will be standing near dancers who are doing the other pattern of movement.

shim sham variation 5

Stand in first position parallel – with the feet parallel but not quite touching and the arms neutral (hanging relaxed at the sides).

> Count and   Step slightly forward on the right heel, and swing the arms slightly forward, keeping them close to the body, with the elbows bent. At the same time, tilt the upper body slightly forward.
>
> 1   Step slightly forward on the left heel, continuing the slight swing of the arms and the forward tilt of the upper body.

Shim Sham Variation 5

and Step back to place with the right foot, placing the ball of the foot on the floor. At the same time, swing the arms downward and slightly past center while straightening the elbows, and lift the chest slightly.

2 Step back to place with the left foot, placing the ball of the foot on the floor. The heel does not touch the floor.

3 Step diagonally forward and to the right with the right foot, and at the same time plié in the right knee and move the arms overhead to cross at the wrists. (See the illustration.) Keep the arms overhead for the remaining counts.

4 Cross the left foot over the right and step there.

5 Step diagonally forward and to the right with the right foot, pliéing in the right knee.

and Bring the left foot next to the right and touch the floor with the ball of the foot.

Repeat on the other side, starting with a slight step forward on the left heel.

Do the exercise with a gliding quality by modifying the footwork slightly. On the first "and" count, for example, let the right foot glide forward a little off the floor so that the step is on the whole foot, not just the heel. Modify the other steps in the same way to maintain the gliding quality.

clAppiNq ExERCisE

Clapping is an important part of rhythmic development. It is often included in jazz dance combinations and sequences, and it has a place in other exercises (see Center Floor Exercise 3 or Catch Step Exercise 4 in this chapter, for instance). Clapping can give a special texture to jazz dance, and syncopation is the key to its use. One way to add clapping to movement is to have the placement of the clap follow the movement, or vice versa. There are many other ways to use clapping. The following is one suggestion only.

Count 1   Step diagonally forward and to the right with the right foot.

and   Clap the hands over the right foot, pointing them in the direction of movement.

2   Step diagonally forward and to the left with the left foot.

and   Clap the hands over the left foot, pointing them in the direction of movement.

3   Step diagonally forward and to the right with the right foot.

and   Clap the hands over the right foot, pointing them in the direction of movement.

4   Clap the hands over the left foot, without moving the foot.

4

isolations

In jazz dance, isolation means the separate movement of one body part while the rest of the body remains still or moves in some other way. The body part isolated at a given time usually provides the main movement at that time, and, of course, it may provide the only movement.

Isolation is one of the basic characteristics of jazz dance, and therefore it is important that students develop sound technique in this kind of movement. The technique should include the ability to emphasize either of two qualities: (1) a smooth and continuous quality, as in a smooth head roll; and (2) a sharp and direct quality, as in a head snap from one side to the other. The smooth and continuous quality is easier to learn, and students should start with it. When they have become familiar with a particular isolation, they are ready to try the sharp and direct quality.

The exercises in this chapter are given in order of difficulty. The number of times each exercise should be done is only a suggestion. Each class will progress at a different rate, and the individuals in the class at individual rates. Further discussion of the way isolation exercises fit into a total class is given in the chapter on class planning.

head isolation 1

Stand in regular second position—with the feet turned out and twelve to twenty-four inches apart—but with the arms and hands in "pressed position." To reach this position, hold the arms directly to the sides and bend the elbows to bring the wrists toward the rib cage until they are

Head Isolation 1

Pressed position

less than two inches from the rib cage. Hold the palms toward the front, extend the fingers and move them apart, and press the heels of the hands forward. (See the illustration.)

Count 1   Look directly to the right side without lifting or dropping the chin. (Focus on an object or place.)

2   Look directly to the left side.

Repeat.

Note: While turning the head from right to left, keep all the other body parts in place. The reason for maintaining the pressed position is to practice this control.

HEAD isolation 2

Stand as in the preceding exercise (with the feet in regular second position and the arms and hands in pressed position).

Count 1   Pull the head directly backward so that the face is parallel to the ceiling.

2   Drop the head directly forward so that the chin is near or touching the top of the chest.

Repeat.

Count 1   Look directly to the right side.

2   Look directly to the left side.

3   Pull the head directly backward (do not return it to center before doing this).

4   Drop the head directly forward.

5   Look directly to the left side.

6   Look directly to the right side.

7   Pull the head directly backward.

8   Drop the head directly forward.

Repeat.

Note: The head should not collapse into position. Rather, the dropping of the head forward and backward should be an action that is completely controlled.

HEAd isolATioN 3

Stand as in Head Isolation 1 (with the feet in regular second position and the arms and hands in pressed position).

Count 1   Drop the head to the right shoulder so that the right ear touches the top of the right shoulder.

2   Drop the head to the left shoulder so that the left ear touches the top of the left shoulder.

Repeat.

Note: The shoulder should not move up to meet the ear. The head should drop as far as possible if it cannot drop all the way to the shoulder.

HEAd isolATioN 4

(Head Roll)

Stand as in Head Isolation 1 (with the feet in regular second position and the arms and hands in pressed position).

Count 1   Drop the head to the right shoulder so that the right ear touches the top of the right shoulder.

2   Pull the head directly backward. (Do not return the head to center.)

3   Drop the head to the left shoulder so that the left ear touches the top of the left shoulder.

4   Drop the head forward so that the chin touches the top of the chest.

Repeat, starting to the left side.

Note: The four directions should eventually be practiced as one continuous circle, taking the head as far in each direction as possible.

Do the head roll in increasing tempos until it becomes possible to circle the head in one count. Alternate sides.

sHouldER isolATioN 1

Stand with the feet in regular second position—with the feet turned out and twelve to twenty-four inches apart—and the arms and hands in pressed position, as described in Head Isolation 1.

Count 1   Lift both shoulders directly upward, as close to the ears as possible.

2   Lower both shoulders, pulling them down toward the floor.

Repeat three times.

Count 1   Lift the right shoulder and pull the left shoulder down toward the floor.

2   Lift the left shoulder and pull the right shoulder down toward the floor.

Repeat five times.

Count 1   Lift the right shoulder and pull the left shoulder down.

and   Lift the left shoulder and pull the right shoulder down.

2-4   Repeat the two counts above, including an "and" count after count 4.

Repeat three times.

sHoulDER isolATioN 2

Stand as in the preceding exercise (with the feet in regular second position and the arms and hands in pressed position).

Count 1   Lift the right shoulder and pull the left shoulder down.

2   Lift the left shoulder and pull the right shoulder down.

3   Lift both shoulders.

and   Drop both shoulders slightly and immediately lift both slightly.

4   Drop both shoulders.

Repeat three times, starting the repetitions by lifting the left shoulder, and alternate sides in succeeding repetitions.

shoulder isolation 3

Stand as in Shoulder Isolation 1 (with the feet in regular second position and the arms and hands in pressed position).

Count 1   Lift the right shoulder and pull the left shoulder down.

and   Drop the right shoulder slightly and then immediately lift both shoulders.

2   Lift the left shoulder slightly and then lift both shoulders again.

3   Lift the right shoulder and drop the left.

and   Drop the right shoulder slightly and then lift both shoulders.

4   Drop both shoulders.

Repeat three times.

Count 1   Move both shoulders directly forward.

and   Move both shoulders directly backward.

2   Move both shoulders directly forward.

3   Move both shoulders directly backward.

and   Move both shoulders directly forward.

4   Move both shoulders directly backward.

Repeat three times.

Note: Do not lift the shoulders to move them freely backward and forward. Instead, maintain a concentrated pull toward the floor.

shoulder isolation 4

(Shoulder Circle)

Stand as in Shoulder Isolation 1 (with the feet in regular second position and the arms and hands in pressed position).

Count 1   Move both shoulders directly forward.

2   Lift both shoulders directly upward.

3   Move both shoulders directly backward.

4   Drop both shoulders directly downward.

Repeat three times.

The following four counts reverse the direction.

Count 1   Move both shoulders directly backward.

2   Lift both shoulders directly upward.

3   Move both shoulders directly forward.

4   Drop both shoulders directly downward.

Repeat three times.

Note: The shoulder circle should be practiced until it can be done as one smooth movement. Advanced students may gradually increase the tempo until they can do a complete shoulder circle in one count.

shouldeR isolation 5

Stand as in Shoulder Isolation 1 (with the feet in regular second position and the arms and hands in pressed position).

Count 1   Circle both shoulders backward: move them upward, backward, downward, and forward.

2   Circle both shoulders backward as in count 1.

3   Move both shoulders directly forward.

and   Move both shoulders directly backward.

4   Move both shoulders slightly forward and immediately lift the right shoulder and drop the left.

and   Lift both shoulders slightly and immediately drop them.

Repeat three times.

shouldeR isolation 6

Stand as in Shoulder Isolation 1 (with the feet in regular second position and the arms and hands in pressed position).

Count 1	Move the right shoulder directly forward and the left shoulder backward.
and	Move the left shoulder directly forward and the right shoulder backward.
a	Move the left shoulder slightly backward and immediately move both shoulders forward.
2	Move both shoulders backward.
3	Circle both shoulders forward: move them forward, upward, backward, and down to place.
and	Circle both shoulders forward *twice*.
a	Lift both shoulders.
4	Drop both shoulders.

shoulder isolation 7

Stand as in Shoulder Isolation 1 (with the feet in regular second position and the arms and hands in pressed position).

Count 1-8	Do the four counts of Shoulder Isolation 5 and follow them with the four counts of Shoulder Isolation 6.
1-8	Reverse the movement; do Shoulder Isolation 6 first.

Repeat three times.

rib cage isolation 1

Stand as in the previous isolation exercises in regular second position—with the feet turned out and twelve to twenty-four inches apart—and the arms and hands in pressed position—that is, with the wrists within two inches of the rib cage, the palms toward the front, the fingers extended and moved apart, and the heels of the hands pressed forward. In addition, lift the rib cage slightly to separate it from the waist.

Count 1	Lift the rib cage directly to the right side.
2	Move the rib cage directly to the center—back to place.

Repeat three times.

Count 1   Lift the rib cage directly to the left side.

      2   Move the rib cage directly to the center – back to place.

      Repeat three times.

Note: The hip should be tightened and the knees kept straight during the rib cage movement to insure no movement from the lower body.

Count 1   Lift the rib cage directly to the right.

      2   Lift the rib cage directly to the left.

      Repeat the two counts four times, moving continuously from right to left and back.

Count1   Move the rib cage directly forward (there will be a slight lift of the chest at the same time).

      2   Move the rib cage back to center (there will be a slight dropping of the chest).

      Repeat four times.

Count 1   Move the rib cage directly backward.

      2   Move the rib cage back to center.

      Repeat four times.

Do a forward movement of the rib cage in one count and then a backward movement of the rib cage in one count. Do not stop at center. Repeat three times.

Rib CAGE isolATioN 2

Stand in second position parallel – with the feet parallel and twelve to twenty-four inches apart – but place the palms on top of the hips and bend the elbows away from the body.

Count 1   Lift the rib cage directly to the right.

      2   Move the rib cage directly forward.

      3   Lift the rib cage directly to the left.

      4   Move the rib cage directly backward.

      Repeat three times.

Do this isolation in alternate directions: move the rib cage to the right, forward, to the left, and backward, as above, and then to the left, forward, to the right, and backward. Repeat three times. Advanced students may do the movement in one smooth and continuous circle.

Rib cage isolation 3

Stand as in the preceding exercise (with the feet in second position parallel, the palms on top of the hips, and the elbows bent away from the body).

Count 1	Lift the rib cage directly to the right.
and	Circle the rib cage forward, to the left, and then backward.
2	Move the rib cage forward.
3	Move the rib cage backward.
4	Move the rib cage forward.
and	Circle the rib cage to the left and then back to center.
Repeat three times.

Do the four counts starting to the left, and repeat three times.

hip isolation 1

Stand in second position parallel — with the feet parallel and twelve to twenty-four inches apart — and add a slight plié in the knees. Hold the arms and hands in pressed position, as in Rib Cage Isolation 1.

Count 1	Contract the hip directly forward.
and	Release the hip back to center.
2	Move the hip directly to the left.
Repeat three times.

Note: When the hip is moved to the side, it will take a slightly upward direction.

| Count 1 | Contract the hip directly forward. |
| 2 | Move the hip directly to the right side. |

3   Release and push the hip directly backward, past center.

4   Move the hip directly to the left side.

Repeat three times.

Do the isolation to the left side on count 2 and to the right on count 4. Repeat three times. Then alternate the sides — first move to the right side on count 2 and next move to the left side on this count — and repeat three times.

Do the four counts in one smooth continuous circle, moving to the right side on count 2. Repeat three times. Advanced students may do the complete hip circle in one count, alternating left and right sides, and repeat the circles three times.

hip isolation 2

Stand as in the preceding exercise (with the feet in second position parallel and the arms and hands in pressed position).

Count 1   Contract the hip directly forward.

2   Move the hip directly to the right.

3   Release and push the hip directly backward, past center.

4   Hold.

Count 1   Contract the hip directly forward.

2   Move the hip directly to the left.

3   Release and push the hip directly backward, past center.

4   Hold.

5   Circle the hip completely around: move it forward, to the left, backward, and to the right.

6   Circle the hip completely around in the other direction: forward, to the right, backward, and to the left.

7   Contract the hip directly forward.

8   Move the hip directly to the right.

Repeat all eight counts three times.

hip isolation 3

Stand as in Hip Isolation 1 (with the feet in second position parallel and the arms and hands in pressed position).

Count 1   Contract the hip directly forward and release.

and   Push the hip slightly backward.

a   Immediately contract the hip slightly forward of center, and release and push the hip directly backward, past center.

2   Contract the hip directly forward.

3   Circle the hip completely around: move it to the left, backward, to the right, and forward.

and   Circle the hip again in the same direction.

a   Release and push the hip directly backward, slightly past center.

4   Push the hip directly backward as far as possible.

Repeat three times.

complex isolation 1

Stand in first position parallel — with the feet parallel but not quite touching. Hold the arms and hands in pressed position — with the wrists within two inches of the rib cage, the palms toward the front, the fingers extended and moved apart, and the heels of the hands pressed forward. Move one body part at a time in the sequence given.

Head

Count 1   Drop the head to the right.

2   Pull the head backward. (Do not return the head to center.)

3   Drop the head to the left.

4   Drop the head forward.

Repeat, starting to the left side.

Shoulders (in half time)

Count 1-2   Circle both shoulders backward: move them upward, backward, downward, and forward.

    3-4   Circle both shoulders backward as in counts 1 and 2.

Count 1-2   Circle both shoulders forward: move them upward, forward, downward, and backward.

    3-4   Circle both shoulders forward again.

Rib Cage

Count 1   Lift the rib cage directly to the right side.

    2   Lift the rib cage directly to the left side.

    3   Lift the rib cage directly to the right side.

    4   Lift the rib cage directly to the left side.

    Repeat.

Hip

Count and   Plié in both knees.

    1   Contract the hip directly forward.

    2   Move the hip directly to the right.

    3   Release and push the hip directly backward, past center.

    4   Move the hip directly to the left.

    Repeat.

Repeat the full sequence three times.

complex isolation 2

Stand in first position parallel with the arms and hands in pressed position, as in the preceding exercise.

Head

Count 1   Circle the head completely around to the right: move it forward, to the right, backward, to the left, and forward again.

       2   Circle the head completely around to the left: move it forward, to the left, backward, to the right, and forward again.

Shoulders

       3   Lift both shoulders and drop both shoulders.

    and   Drop both shoulders farther.

       4   Move both shoulders forward.

    and   Move both shoulders back to center.

       a   Plié in both knees.

Hip

       5   Contract the hip directly forward, release the hip backward, and immediately contract the hip forward again.

    and   Release and push the hip directly backward.

       6   Contract the hip directly forward.

    and   Release the hip backward to center and straighten the knees.

Repeat the full sequence three times.

complex isolation 3

Stand in first position parallel with the arms and hands in pressed position, as in the preceding complex isolations.

Head

Count 1   Snap the head to look to the right, and return it to center.

       2   Snap the head to look to the left, and return it to center.

Shoulders

3	Move both shoulders forward.
and	Move both shoulders backward.
4	Lift both shoulders and drop them back to center.

Rib Cage

5	Lift the rib cage directly to the right, to the left, and then back to center.
and	Plié in both knees.

Hip

6	Circle the hip completely around: move it to the right, backward, to the left, and to center.
and	Straighten the knees.

Repeat the full sequence three times.

complex isolation 4

Stand in first position parallel with the arms and hands in pressed position, as in the preceding complex isolations.

Head

Count 1	Circle the head completely around to the right: move it to the right, backward, to the left, and forward.
and	Again circle the head completely around to the right, ending on center after the move forward.

Shoulders

a	Lift both shoulders.

2   Drop both shoulders and at the same time move the right shoulder backward and the left shoulder forward.

3   Move the right shoulder forward and the left shoulder backward.

and Move the right shoulder backward and the left shoulder forward.

a   Move both shoulders back to center.

Rib Cage

4   Move the rib cage directly backward.

and Move the rib cage to center again.

5   Plié in both knees.

Hip

and Move the hip directly to the right.

6   Move the hip to center again.

and Straighten the knees.

Repeat the full sequence three times.

complex isolation 5

Stand in first position parallel with the arms and hands in pressed position as in the preceding complex isolations.

Head

Count 1 Drop the head directly forward.

2   Drop the head to the left. (Do not return the head to center.)

3   Pull the head backward.

4   Drop the head to the right.

5   Drop the head forward.

6   Drop the head to the right.

7   Drop the head backward.

8   Drop the head to the left and then to center.

Shoulders

1   Move the right shoulder backward and the left shoulder forward.

2   Move the right shoulder forward and the left shoulder backward.

3   Circle both shoulders backward, upward, forward, and downward.

4   Again circle both shoulders backward, upward, forward, and downward, ending on center after the move downward.

5   Move the right shoulder forward and the left shoulder backward.

6   Move the left shoulder forward and the right shoulder backward.

7   Circle both shoulders forward, upward, backward, and downward.

8   Again circle both shoulders forward, upward, backward, and downward, ending on center after the move downward.

Rib Cage

1   Move the rib cage directly forward.

2   Move the rib cage directly backward, past center.

3   Lift the rib cage directly to the left.

4   Lift the rib cage directly to the right and then to center.

5   Move the rib cage directly forward.

6	Move the rib cage directly backward.
7	Lift the rib cage directly to the right.
8	Lift the rib cage directly to the left and then back to center.

Hip

1	Plié in both knees.
and	Move the hip directly backward.
2	Contract the hip directly forward.
3	Release and push the hip directly backward, past center.
and	Contract the hip directly forward.
4	Circle the hip completely around: to the right, backward, to the left, and forward.
5	Circle the hip again as in count 4.
6	Circle the hip again as in count 4.
and	Release the hip to center.
7	Move the hip directly to the right.
8	Move the hip directly to the left.
and	Move the hip to center and straighten the knees.

Repeat the full sequence three times.

complex isolation 6

Stand in first position parallel with the arms and hands in pressed position, as in the preceding complex isolations.

Head

Count 1	Drop the head to the right shoulder.
and	Move the head *toward* center a little.
a	Drop the head *toward* the right a little and then return the head *toward* center, so that the head is still tilted slightly.

2   Drop the head to the right shoulder.

and   Move the head directly to the left shoulder, past center.

a   Move the head *toward* center.

3   Drop the head to the left shoulder.

4   Move the head directly to the right shoulder, past center.

5   Drop the head forward.

and   Pull the head *toward* the back.

a   Drop the head *toward* the front.

6   Pull the head backward, past center.

7   Drop the head forward, past center.

8   Return the head to center.

Shoulders

1   Move the right shoulder forward and the left shoulder backward.

and   Move the right shoulder slightly backward.

a   Move the right shoulder slightly backward again, and move the left shoulder slightly forward.

2   Move the right shoulder all the way back and the left shoulder all the way forward.

3   Move the right shoulder forward and the left shoulder backward.

4   Move the left shoulder forward and the right shoulder backward.

5   Lift both shoulders.

and   Drop both shoulders slightly.

a   Drop both shoulders slightly more.

6   Drop both shoulders.

7   Move the right shoulder backward and the left shoulder forward, and circle the shoulders: move the right shoulder

backward, upward, forward, and downward; and move the
left shoulder forward, upward, backward, and downward.

8 Move the right shoulder forward and the left shoulder
backward, and circle the shoulders: move the right
shoulder forward, upward, backward, and downward; and
move the left shoulder backward, upward, forward, and
downward.

Rib Cage

1 Move the rib cage directly forward.

and Move the rib cage slightly backward.

a Move the rib cage farther backward.

2 Move the rib cage all the way back.

and Move the rib cage slightly forward.

a Move the rib cage farther forward.

3 Move the rib cage all the way forward.

4 Move the rib cage all the way back.

5 Lift the rib cage to the right.

and Move the rib cage *toward* center slightly.

a Move the rib cage farther *toward* center.

6 Lift the rib cage all the way to the left.

7 Lift the rib cage to the right.

8 Lift the rib cage to the left and then back to center.

Hips

1 Plié in both knees.

and Move the hip *toward* the right.

a Move the hip farther *toward* the right.

2 Move the hip all the way to the right.

and Move the hip all the way to the left.

Isolations

a	Move the hip to center.
3	Push the hip backward.
4	Contract the hip forward.
5	Circle the hip completely around: move it to the right, backward, to the left, and then forward.
and	Circle the hip again as in count 5.
a	Release the hip to center.
6	Push the hip backward.
7	Contract the hip forward.
8	Release and push the hip backward, and then bring it to center.

Repeat the full sequence three times.

5

TURNS

A number of common jazz dance turns are described in this chapter. The turns are selected ones. It is important to realize that there are other turns, including those that evolve from a particular experience with music. Like the preceding chapters, this one presents its material in order of difficulty, from simple to complex, and the choice of material should depend on the needs of a class. Following the center floor turns is a series of four-count turns that is good for beginners, and this series is followed by special turns.

For the most part, the turns described do not require the ability to spot. However, the parallel turn (Special Turn 1) does necessitate some practice in spotting.

One of the simple ways to approach spotting is as follows: Stand with the right side of the body toward the front, the feet and arms in second position – that is, with the feet turned out and twelve to twenty-four inches apart and with the arms extended to the sides – and the head turned to the right (facing front). Make a half turn to the right, but keep the head focused on the same spot. Then make another half turn to the right, this time snapping the head completely around on the "and" count and letting the body follow. Focus the eyes forward without lifting or dropping the chin at a natural level and at a specific object – real or imagined – on the wall or in space. During the turn, the arms move from second position on the first step into the turn with the right foot, to a closed position in front of the chest – with the elbows bent approximately a foot away from the chest – as the step is taken with the left foot.

When the half turn and head snap are mastered, gradually increase the speed of turning.

Another important technique is that of landing from a jump. During Center Floor Turn 7, for instance, there is a time when the foot leaves the floor in a hop, and the landing should be done correctly. To learn how to land, stand in first position parallel — that is, with the feet parallel and nearly touching and the arms neutral (hanging relaxed at the sides). Do several pliés with the heels on the floor. Then do pliés and straighten the knees to move to a half-toe position after each plié. When coming down from half-toe, pay particular attention to the articulation of the foot, moving from the ball of the foot to the center and finally to a cushioning of the plié with the heel. Once both kinds of pliés have become familiar, take small jumps from the floor, landing all the way from the ball of the foot through the heel into a plié. Concentrate on a proper landing.

Turns should be learned in the context of a total sequence of movement, as opposed to stress on one or a few turns only. Learning may be aided by appropriate footwear, including shoes with leather soles, gymnastic slippers, ballet shoes, or practice socks (when using socks, be certain the floor surface is not too slippery).

center floor turn 1

Stand in an easy (relaxed) first position parallel — feet parallel and nearly touching and arms neutral. Plié in both knees. The exercise begins with practice in moving to the right without a turn.

Count 1	Step to the right about six inches with the right foot, and swing the arms backward easily from the neutral position.
2	Step with the left foot to place it next to the right, and swing the arms easily forward.
3	Step to the right about six inches with the right foot, and swing the arms easily backward.
4	Step with the left foot next to the right, but place only the ball of the foot on the floor, and keep most of the weight on the right foot. Swing the arms easily to neutral position.

Repeat to the left, starting on the left foot.

Count 1   Step to the right as in count 1 above, adding a quarter turn to the right.

2   Step with the left foot as in count 2 above, adding another quarter turn to the right to face opposite the starting position.

3   Step to the right again as in count 1, with a quarter turn to the right.

4   Step with the left foot as in count 4 above, adding a quarter turn to end facing front with the ball of the left foot on the floor, but most of the weight on the right foot.

Repeat to the left, starting with the left foot.

Note: The amount of space covered can vary from one side to the other, but students should strive to increase the space gradually on either side, and at the same time to increase the tempo.

CENTER floor turn 2

Stand in an easy first position parallel and plié in both knees, as in the previous exercise. Repeat the turning steps of the previous exercise, and add the following arm movement.

Count 1   Begin to turn the fingertips upward while bending the elbows to bring the lower arms upward close to the body, with the palms touching or close to the rib cage.

2   Continue to lift the lower arms until they are up to the shoulder.

3   Extend both arms fully to form a V overhead.

4   Turn the palms away from the body and open the V.

Repeat the turning steps to the left, and at the same time reverse the arm movement so that the lower arms and hands lead downward in front of the shoulders and beside the rib cage to return to neutral.

Note: The arm movement should be a smooth, continuous action.

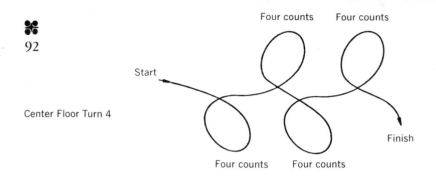

Center Floor Turn 4

CENTER floor TURN 3

Stand in an easy first position parallel and plié in both knees, as before. This exercise repeats the steps of Center Floor Turn 1 in two new directions: forward and back.

Count 1   Step forward about six inches with the right foot, and swing the arms easily backward.

2   Step with the left foot to place it next to the right, and swing the arms easily forward.

3   Step forward about six inches with the right foot, and swing the arms easily backward.

4   Step with the left foot next to the right, but place only the ball of the left foot on the floor and keep most of the weight on the right foot.

Repeat moving backward, starting on the left foot.

Do the steps in all four directions: move right, left, forward, and backward, in order. Take four counts for each direction.

Do the steps in four directions with four turns. Move to the right and turn to the right, beginning on the right foot. Then move to the left and turn to the left, beginning on the left foot. Move forward and turn to the right, beginning on the right foot, and finally move backward and turn to the left, beginning on the left foot.

Do the four turns and add the arm movement described in Center Floor Turn 2.

CENTER floor TURN 4

Stand in an easy first position parallel and plié in both knees. This exercise repeats the turning steps of Center Floor Turn 1 in diagonal directions, alternating steps forward and to the right with steps forward and to the left. (See the illustration.)

Count 1   Step diagonally forward and to the right about six inches with the right foot while taking a quarter turn to the right.

2   Step with the left foot to place it next to the right, taking another quarter turn to the right.

3   Step again with the right foot to move in the same direction as in count 1, taking another quarter turn to the right.

4   Step with the left foot next to the right, with the ball of the left foot on the floor but with most of the weight on the right foot, taking a final quarter turn to end facing forward, as at the beginning of count 1.

Repeat while moving diagonally to the left, starting on the left foot and turning to the left.

Do the alternating diagonal steps and add the arm movement described in Center Floor Turn 2.

Do the steps and arm movement and add a head action: on each count 4, drop the head directly backward, and bring it forward to place on the "and" count before count 1.

CENTER FLOOR TURN 5

Stand in an easy first position parallel and plié in both knees. This exercise completes a diagonal turn in three counts rather than the four of the preceding exercise.

Count 1   Step diagonally forward and to the right about six inches with the right foot while taking a quarter turn to the right.

2   Step with the left foot to place it next to the right while taking a half turn to the right.

3   Complete the turn by taking a quarter turn on the right foot and bringing the left foot in next to the right, with most of the weight on the right.

4   Hold.

Repeat while moving diagonally left, starting on the left foot and turning to the left.

Do the alternating diagonal turns in three counts and add a head drop

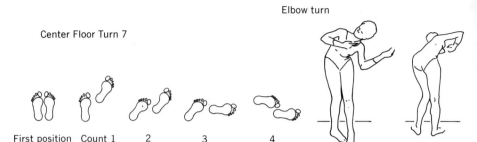

Center Floor Turn 7

Elbow turn

First position   Count 1   2   3   4

on count 4: drop the head directly backward on the count and bring it forward to place on the next "and" count, as in the preceding exercise.

CENTER floor turn 6

Stand in an easy first position parallel — with the feet parallel and nearly touching and with the arms neutral (hanging relaxed at the sides) — and plié in both knees, as in the previous exercises. The footwork in this exercise is identical to that of Center Floor Turn 1 until the "and" count after count 3. Like Center Floor Turn 1, this exercise begins with practice in moving without a turn.

Count 1   Step to the right about six inches with the right foot.

2   Step with the left foot to place it next to the right.

3   Step to the right about six inches with the right foot.

and   Step with the left foot next to the right, but place only the ball of the foot on the floor, and keep most of the weight on the right foot.

4   Step backward and diagonally left about twenty-four inches with the left foot, placing the left toe on the floor. At the same time, deepen the plié on the right side.

Repeat to the left, starting on the left foot.

Do the steps described above and add the arm movement described in Center Floor Turn 2. Then repeat the steps with a turn:

Count 1   Step to the right about six inches with the right foot and add a quarter turn to the right.

2   Step with the left foot to place it next to the right and take a half turn to the right.

3   Step to the right again as in count 1, adding a quarter turn to the right.

and   Step with the left foot next to the right, but place only the ball of the foot on the floor, and keep most of the weight on the right foot.

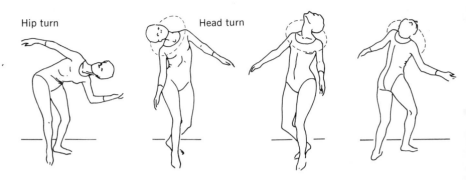

Hip turn   Head turn

4   Step backward and diagonally left about twenty-four inches with the left foot, placing the left toe on the floor. At the same time, deepen the plié on the right side.

Repeat to the left, turning to the left and starting on the left foot.

Note: Accentuate counts 3 and "and" by making them stronger than the others.

CENTER floor TURN 7

(Paddle Turn Series)

Stand in first position parallel and plié in both knees.

Count 1   Lift the right foot slightly off the floor — just enough so that it doesn't touch — and put it down with a slight turn to the right. (See the illustrations of foot positions.)

2   Lift the left foot slightly off the floor and put it down with another slight turn to the right.

3   Repeat count 1.

4   Repeat count 2.

Note: The paddle turn is the basis for a series of turns that are initiated from various parts of the body. These turns are begun with the right side of the body facing front. Once the initiating body part — elbow, hip, or head — causes other body parts to fall away from center, these parts must be held in position. For example, during the elbow turn the upper body and head are directed to the left side in relation to the elbows as the turn starts, and they must stay in this position, without collapsing, during the turn. Once the paddle turn can be done in various tempos — slow, medium, and fast — the other turns may be learned.

Do an *elbow turn* to the right by bending both elbows to the right in front of the chest. This initiates a bend of the upper body to the left. Plié and let the elbows lead the rest of the body in the turn, supported by a paddle turn. Repeat to the left side. (See the illustrations.)

Do a *hip turn* to the right by extending the right hip to the right. Plié and place the arms in second position (extended to the sides) but with

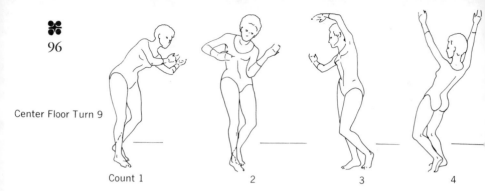

Center Floor Turn 9

Count 1   2   3   4

the left elbow slightly bent and the left palm upward. The hip leads the turn, which is supported by a paddle turn. Repeat to the left side. (See the illustration.)

Do a *head turn* to the right by dropping the head forward, to the right, and then back. At the point of taking the head back, pull the rest of the body into the turn, with the knees in plié and the arms neutral on a paddle turn base. Make the head circle as one continuous motion. (See the illustrations.)

CENTER floor turn 8

(Pivot Turn)

Stand in an easy first position parallel and plié in both knees.

Count and   Hop on the left foot, landing on the whole foot (the ball, center, and heel in quick succession) and immediately lifting the heel off the floor. At the same time, begin to lift the arms sideward and upward, toward second position.

1   Cross the right foot over the left so that the ankles are close together and both heels are off the floor. Plié. Lift the arms to second position and bend the upper body to the right.

2   Pivot to the left, keeping the upper body bent.

3   Continue pivoting to the left.

4   Continue pivoting to end facing front, and return the upper body to center.

Repeat on the right side, turning to the right.

Do the exercise without bending the upper body on count 1. Instead, deepen the plié as much as possible, keeping the torso centered.

Do the exercise with both a bending of the upper body and a deepening of the plié on count 1.

Do the exercise with a bending of the upper body to the left, right, and left on counts 2, 3, and 4. Then do the bending to explore different rhythmic variations during these counts.

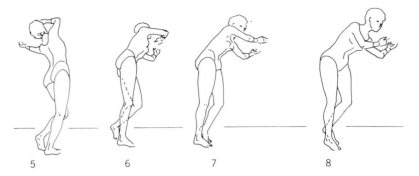

5   6   7   8

CENTER floor TURN 9

(Spiral Turn)

Stand in first position parallel with the right side toward the line of direction, and plié in both knees. The spiral turn here requires sixteen paddle turn steps for each spiral; there are many other spiral turns. (See the illustrations.)

Count 1   Lift the right foot slightly off the floor and step forward and right to begin a spiral to the right while doing a paddle turn to the right. Lift the left foot and step to continue the spiral and the turn. At the same time, start to bend the upper body forward from the waist and bend the elbows to the right as the arms move forward.

2   Step with the right foot and the left foot to complete a quarter turn, at the same time bending farther forward and lifting the arms slightly toward the right shoulder.

3   Step with the right foot and the left foot again, bending the upper body to the right and continuing to lift the arms.

4   Step with the right foot and the left foot to finish a half turn, at the same time bending the upper body backward and completing the lift of the arms so that the elbows are straight and the palms are toward each other.

5   Step right and left to begin a second half turn, continuing to travel in a spiral, and bend the upper body to the left side, letting the arms follow.

6   Step right and left again, bending the upper body forward and letting the arms follow.

7   Step right and left, bending the upper body toward center and letting the arms follow.

8   Step right and left to complete the spiral and the second turn, bending the upper body back to center.

Note: The second circle of the upper body, on counts 5 through 8, is performed at a higher level than the first.

Do the spiral turn in a faster count of eight or in a slow count of four.

CENTER floor TURN 10

(Combination Three-Step and Turn)

Stand in first position parallel with the arms neutral (hanging relaxed at the sides). Plié slightly in both knees.

Count 1
    Step directly forward with the right foot. Lift the arms toward second position (extended to the sides), but move the left arm forward and the right arm diagonally backward.

2
    Step with the left foot to place it slightly behind the right, with only the ball of the left foot touching the floor. At the same time, move the right arm forward and the left arm backward.

3
    Step directly forward with the right foot, and move the left arm forward and the right arm backward.

1
    Shift the weight to the left foot and step directly to the right side with the right foot. Move the arms to second position and hold them there until the end of count 4.

2
    Step with the left foot, making a half turn to the right.

3
    Step with the right foot, making another half turn to the right to face front again.

4
    Step with the left foot to place it next to the right, with only the ball of the left foot touching the floor. Return the arms to neutral.

Repeat the combination on the left side, starting forward on the left foot and then turning to the left after the first three counts.

Note: Maintain the slight plié throughout the combination.

CENTER floor TURN 11

(Combination Three-Step and Pivot Turn)

Stand in first position parallel with the arms neutral, and plié slightly in both knees.

Count 1-3   Step directly forward with the right foot and bring the left foot slightly behind the right, stepping on the ball of the left foot. Then step forward again with the right foot, as in the first three counts of Center Floor Turn 10.

1-3   Repeat these counts on the other side, stepping left, right, left.

and   Hop on the left foot, landing on the whole foot (the ball, center, and heel in quick succession) and immediately lift the heel off the floor. At the same time, begin to lift the arms sideward and upward, toward second position.

1   Repeat the pivot turn to the left in four counts described as Center Floor Turn 8. On this count, cross the right foot over the left so that the ankles are close together and both heels are off the floor. Plié. Lift the arms to second position and bend the upper body to the right.

2   Pivot to the left, keeping the upper body bent.

3   Continue pivoting to the left.

4   Continue pivoting to end facing front, and return the upper body to center.

Repeat the combination on the other side, starting a three-step on the left foot, doing another three-step that starts on the right foot, then hopping on the right foot and doing a pivot turn to the right.

CENTER floor turn 12

(Combination Four-Step and Turn)

Stand in first position parallel with the arms neutral, and plié deeply in both knees.

Count 1   Step diagonally forward and to the right on the right foot, and move the arms sideward and upward to second position.

2   Step forward on the left foot to place it next to the right, stepping on the whole foot. At the same time, move the

Center Floor Turn 12

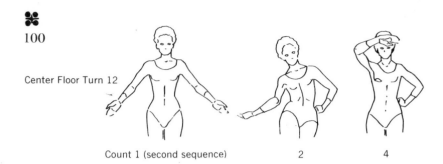

Count 1 (second sequence)   2   4

arms downward in front of the hip so that they cross at the wrists.

3   Step diagonally forward and to the right on the right foot, and continue the motion of the arms by bringing them across each other and up overhead.

4   Step with the left foot to bring it to place next to the right, with only the ball of the left foot touching the floor, and continue the motion of the arms by opening them sideward and downward toward waist level.

Count 1   Step to the left side with the left foot, and continue to move both arms downward to slightly below waist level. (See the illustration.)

2   Take a half turn to the left with the right foot. At the same time, bend the left elbow and place the top of the left hand — the palm is closed — on the left hip, while continuing to lower the right arm with the palm toward the back so that the elbow is leading the right arm forward. (See the illustration.)

3   Take a half turn to the left with the left foot, and continue the movement of the right arm forward and upward.

and   Step with the right foot to place it close to the left, with only the ball of the right foot touching the floor, and continue to lift the right arm.

4   Step diagonally backward and to the right about twenty-four inches with the right foot. At the same time, continue to lift the right arm until the lower arm is slightly in front of the forehead and the palm is toward the floor. (See the illustration.)

Note: The "and" count is accented.

CENTER floor turn 13

(Rhythm Turn)

Stand in first position parallel with the arms neutral. Plié deeply in both knees.

Count 1   Step forward and diagonally right with the right foot.

2   Take a half turn to the right with the left foot.

3   Take a half turn to the right with the right foot.

and   Move the hip directly to the left side, lifting the heel of the left foot off the floor and pliéing deeper in the left knee.

4   Move the hip directly to the right side, lifting the heel of the right foot off the floor and pliéing deeper in the right knee.

Repeat, moving diagonally backward and to the left and turning to the left.

CENTER floor TURN 14
(Rhythm Turn with Arm Movement)

Stand in first position parallel with the arms neutral, and plié deeply in both knees. Repeat the steps of the previous turn, adding the following arm movement.

Count 1   Rotate the wrists backward so that the palms are toward the front with the elbows bent, and begin to lift the palms upward.

2   Continue to lift the palms with the elbows bent and the arms close to the body.

3   Continue to lift the palms until they are overhead with the elbows straight and the arms in a V.

and   Continue to lift the palms.

a   Continue the lifting until the palms are overhead with the elbows straight and the arms in a V.

4   Rotate the arms so that the palms are toward the floor and open the arms to form a wider V.

Repeat the arm movement while moving diagonally backward and to the left and turning to the left.

fOUR—COUNT TURN 1

Stand in an easy (relaxed) second position with turn out to the left side — that is, with the feet twelve to twenty-four inches apart, with the left foot pointed to the left, and with the arms extended to the sides. Shift most of the weight to the left foot. Do not plié.

Count 1   Step to the right with the right foot, taking a quarter turn to the right. Hold the arms in second position throughout the four counts.

   2   Step to the right with the left foot, taking another quarter turn to the right.

   3   Step with the right foot to take a half turn to the right, completing the turn.

   4   Move the left foot out to the left to resume second position with turn out.

Repeat, starting with the left foot and turning to the left.

fOUR—COUNT TURN 2

Stand in an easy second position with turn out to the left side, and shift most of the weight to the left foot.

Count 1-3   Repeat the first three counts of the previous exercise.

   4   Move the left foot out to the left to resume second position with turn out, and at the same time bend the left elbow to bring the lower arm to the chest, with the palm toward the chest and with the fingers open and straight. Then return the left arm to second position.

Repeat all four counts, starting with the left foot and turning to the left, and moving the right arm on count 4.

fOUR—COUNT TURN 3

Stand in an easy second position with turn out to the left side, and shift most of the weight to the left foot.

Count 1-3 Repeat the first three counts of Four-Count Turn 1.

4 Bend the left elbow to bring the lower arm to the chest, with the palm toward the chest and the fingers open and straight, as in Four-Count Turn 2. At the same time, shift most of the weight to the right foot and plié in the right knee. Then plié in the left knee, with only the ball of the left foot touching the floor.

and Straighten the knees, resume the turn out, and return the left arm to second position.

Repeat on the opposite side, starting with the left foot and turning to the left, and moving the right arm on count 4 and the "and" count following.

FOUR-COUNT TURN 4

Stand in an easy second position with turn out, and shift most of the weight to the left foot.

Count 1-3 Repeat the first three counts of Four-Count Turn 1.

4 Plié deeply in the right knee and at the same time cross the left foot behind the right, diagonally backward and to the right. Simultaneously reach with both arms diagonally backward and to the right, toward the floor, letting the arms pull the entire torso backward with a diagonal line from the head to the hip. Hold the arms about eighteen inches apart at the wrists, in front of the body, at the end of the reaching movement.

and Straighten the right knee and bring the body back to center and at the same time bring the arms and the left leg back to second position.

Repeat on the opposite side, starting with the left foot and turning to the left, and reaching both arms to the left and pliéing and straightening in the left knee on count 4 and on the "and" count following.

four-count turn 5

Stand in an easy second position with turn out, and shift most of the weight to the left foot.

Count 1-3 Repeat the first three counts of Four-Count Turn 1.

4 Repeat count 4 of Four-Count Turn 4.

and Open the arms to second position and lift the left leg to the left side as high as possible. Straighten the right knee to resume second position with turn out as the left foot returns to the floor.

Repeat on the opposite side, starting with the left foot and turning to the left, reaching both arms to the left while pliéing in the left knee on count 4, and opening both arms while lifting the right leg to the right side on the "and" count following.

four-count turn 6

Stand in an easy second position with turn out, and shift most of the weight to the left foot.

Count 1-3 Repeat the first three counts of Four-Count Turn 1.

4 Repeat count 4 of Four-Count Turn 4.

5 Begin a spiral turn by bending the upper body to the left side and bring the arms across the front of the body until they reach diagonally left and backward toward the floor. At the same time, take a quarter turn to the right with the right foot, as in count 1.

6 Take a quarter turn to the right with the left foot, as in count 2, and let the upper body and arms follow, with the arms moving diagonally up on either side of the head and the elbows straight.

7 Take a half turn to the right with the right foot, as in count 3, and continue to let the upper body and arms follow in an upward spiral.

8   Move the left foot out to the left and straighten the right knee to resume second position with turn out to the left side. At the same time bring the upper body back to center and open the arms downward and sideward to second position.

Repeat all eight counts on the opposite side, turning to the left.

fOUR—COUNT TURN 7

Stand in an easy second position with turn out to the left side, and shift most of the weight to the left foot.

Count 1-3   Repeat the first three counts of Four-Count Turn 1.

4   Repeat count 4 of Four-Count Turn 4.

5   Move the upper body to the left side, bringing the arms across the front of the body until they reach diagonally left and backward toward the floor, as in count 5 of the preceding exercise, but do not turn with the feet.

6   Circle the upper body backward and upward, with the arms on either side of the head and the elbows straight. At the same time, pivot to the left, stepping with the left foot.

7   Continue the upward spiral of the upper body and continue pivoting to the left, stepping with the right foot.

8   Complete the pivot turn and move the left foot out to the left to resume second position with turn out to the left side. At the same time bring the upper body back to center and open the arms downward to second position.

Repeat all eight counts on the opposite side, turning first to the left and then to the right.

spEciAl TURN 1

(Parallel Turn)

Stand in first position parallel — that is, with the feet parallel and nearly touching and the arms neutral (hanging relaxed at the sides). Begin by practicing the arm movement only. The complete parallel turn requires some practice in spotting, as described at the beginning of the chapter.

Count 1   Lift both arms, moving the left arm directly forward while the right arm lifts at the side, and rotate the arms so that the palms are toward each other.

2   Bend both elbows *sharply,* bring the lower arms to the chest. Hold the fingers straight and open, with the palms toward the chest and no more than one or two inches away.

Reverse the arms, moving the right arm forward while lifting the left arm at the side.

Note: The elbows must remain parallel to the floor at all times, and the movement on count 2 must be stronger than on count 1.

Count 1   Repeat the arm movement of count 1 and at the same time step twelve inches forward with the right foot, leaving the ball of the left foot on the floor. Move the entire body forward over the right foot.

2   Let the movement of the arms initiate the turn. Lift the right heel off the floor slightly and pivot to the left, lifting the ball of the left foot off the floor and bringing the lower left leg to a position parallel to the floor.

Repeat on the opposite side, stepping forward on the left foot and turning to the right.

Note: Do not bring the left knee forward during the turn, and remain in a plié throughout the turn.

Do the turn at gradually increasing tempos. Advanced students may attempt two turns in the two counts.

special turn 2

(Running Turn)

Stand in first position parallel with the arms neutral, and plié in both knees.

Count 1   Take a running step forward with the right foot.

2   Take a running step forward with the left foot.

3   Jump into second position — with the feet twelve to twenty-four inches apart — placing the feet in a slight turn out and pliéing deeper than before.

4   Hop on the left foot and at the same time lift the right knee so that the lower right leg is on a diagonal line in front of the left leg.

5   Jump into second position with both feet.

6   Hop on the left foot and lift the right knee, as in count 4, only this time turn all the way around to the right to end in first position parallel.

Repeat, beginning again with the right foot and turning to the right, and then repeat several times beginning with the left foot and turning to the left.

special turn 3

(Running Turn with Arm Movement)

Stand in first position parallel with the arms neutral, and plié in both knees. Repeat the steps of the previous exercise and add the following arm movement.

Count 1   Swing the right arm forward and the left arm forward.

2   Swing the right arm forward and low and the left arm backward and low.

3   Move both arms to a low second position — with the hands and arms extended to the sides at about waist level.

4   Bend the left elbow and bring it toward the waist, with the palm toward the back and near the rib cage. Hold the right arm extended as at the end of count 3.

5   Straighten the left elbow to return the left arm to low second position.

6   Move the arms to an even lower second position, so that a

diagonal line runs from either shoulder to the fingers, which are about eighteen inches from the hip.

Repeat on the opposite side.

Do the running turn starting with the right foot, but instead of lifting the right knee on count 6, extend the right leg forward and parallel to the floor with the foot flexed and the arms lifted to a regular second position.

special turn 4

(Air Turn)

Stand in first position parallel with the arms neutral and plié slightly in both knees. The impetus of an air turn—done with both feet off the floor—is the natural spring an individual has. The turn should be preceded by a warm-up consisting of small jumps, with the feet articulated properly, and progressing gradually to higher jumps until each student is jumping as high as possible.

Count and	Jump forward.
1	Land.
and	Plié and jump forward.
2	Land.
and	Plié and jump forward.
3	Land.
and	Plié and jump up, at the same time taking a half turn to the right to end facing backward.
4	Land.
and	Plié and jump in the direction faced (moving opposite the direction of the preceding jumps).
1	Land.
and	Plié and jump in the direction faced.
2	Land.
and	Plié and jump in the direction faced.

3 Land.

and Plié and jump up, at the same time taking a half turn to the right to end facing in the original direction.

4 Land.

special turn 5

(Low Turn)

Stand with the feet in first position parallel and the arms in second position (extended to the sides).

Count 1 Step diagonally forward and to the right with the right foot, pliéing in both knees.

  2 Take a half turn to the right with the left foot, deepening the plié in both knees.

  3 Take a half turn to the right on the right foot to end facing front, and deepen the plié further.

  4 Bring the left knee in close to the right (the left knee now almost touches the floor).

  Repeat, starting on the left foot and turning to the left.

Do the low turn with a gradual lowering of the arms. When turning to the right, bring the arms diagonally downward and to the right so that the left hand is brought to the right side of the waist and the right arm is brought behind the lower back, with the hand ending on the left side of the waist. Reverse the arm movement when turning to the left.

wAlks ANd combiNATioNs

Jazz walks and movement combinations demand practice and skill development if they are to be done well. At the same time, these advanced exercises offer scope for the expression of individual style.

Four of the combinations in the chapter, "Masquenada," "Along Comes Mary," "Grazing in the Grass," and "Cold Sweat" are named for specific records, and the music of these records should be used in teaching. The first three combinations named are designed to go with music by the South African trumpeter Hugh Masekela. "Masquenada" is on the albums "All-Time Hits of Hugh Masekela" (GAS 116, MGM) and "Americanization of Ooga Booga" (MGM S-4372). "Along Comes Mary" is also on "All-Time Hits of Hugh Masekela" as well as on "Next Album" (MGM S-4415). "Grazing in the Grass" is on "The Best of Hugh Masekela" (UNI 7305-1) and on the two-record set "Promise of a Future" (UNI 73028). The final combination, "Cold Sweat," is designed to go with music by Mongo Santamaria which is available on "Heavy Sounds" (Columbia CS 99-70), "Mongo Santamaria's Greatest Hits" (Columbia CS-1060), and "Soul Bag" (Columbia CS-9653).

The movements that follow progress from relatively easy to quite complex, and these movements should be coordinated with the exercises in the previous chapters to suit the needs of particular classes. The number of repetitions of each exercise must depend on circumstances. For example, the "Masquenada" combination and its variations may be done separately, or as a single developmental sequence with the theme and variations each performed four times on a side and then repeated on the other side.

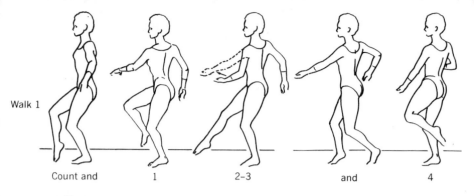

Walk 1

| Count and | 1 | 2-3 | and | 4 |

WAlk 1

(Basic Jazz Walk)

Stand in a modified first position parallel – that is, place the feet comfortably apart (no more than four inches) with a slight turn out, and hold the arms neutral. Plié in both knees. (See the illustrations.)

Count and Lift the right foot slightly off the floor and up toward the right hip, and bend the left elbow slightly away from the body, with the palm toward the body.

1 Continue to lift the right foot by raising the knee, and continue to bend the left elbow away from the body.

2 Begin to extend the right leg forward from the knee, and begin to turn the left palm toward the ceiling, with the little finger moving toward the side of the body. At the same time, begin to lift the right elbow away from the body.

3 Continue to extend the right leg forward from the knee until the knee is almost straight and the left heel is slightly off the floor. At the same time, begin to extend the lower left arm and continue to lift the right elbow.

and Shift the body weight forward, toward the right foot, by pushing off from the left heel and lifting the heel slightly off the floor. At the same time extend the lower left arm forward until the elbow is practically straight and continue to lift the right elbow, turning the palm over to face the ceiling.

4 Step on the right foot, shifting the weight farther forward so that the left foot is slightly off the floor, and begin to lower the left arm toward the floor while extending the right arm forward.

Repeat on the opposite side, stepping with the left foot.

Note: This walk can be done with many qualities. The two that are most important to develop are (1) a smooth, continuous quality and (2) a sharp quality.

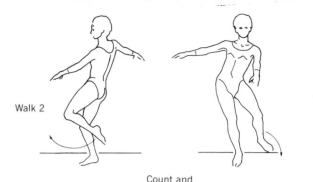

Walk 2

Count and

wAlk 2

(Strut Walk)

Stand in an easy first position parallel with the arms neutral, and plié in both knees. Keep the plié throughout the walk.

Count 1   Step forward on the right foot and at the same time lift the left foot slightly backward while swinging the right arm sideward and the left arm forward.

and   Lift the right heel and put it down. At the same time bring the left foot forward on a circular path: backward, to the left, and forward, and complete the swing of the arms. (See the two illustrations of this "and" count.)

2   Step on the left foot in front and at the same time lift the right foot slightly backward while reversing the armswing.

and   Lift the left heel and put it down. At the same time bring the right foot forward on a circular path: backward, to the right, and forward, and complete the swing of the arms.

Repeat.

Note: In this walk the quality should be like that of a skater with an added bounce. The entire body should bounce as a unit, and the walk should be done as one continuous movement.

wAlk 3

(Afro-Cuban Walk)

Stand in a modified first position parallel, with the feet comfortably apart (no more than four inches) and slightly turned out. Plié slightly in both knees and maintain the plié throughout the walk. Hold the arms with the elbows and lower arms lifted at about waist level, with the palms away from the body and with the hands and fingers slightly curved so that the thumb touches the forefinger.

Count 1   Step forward on the right foot and immediately lift the left foot off the floor in back. At the same time push the right hip forward, to the right, and back to center, in a half

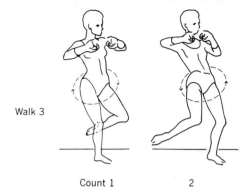

Walk 3

Count 1   2

circle. Move the knee and hip as a single unit during the half circle. (See the illustration.)

2   Step forward on the left foot and immediately lift the right foot off the floor in back. At the same time push the left hip in a half circle forward, to the left, and back to center. (See the illustration.)

Repeat.

COMBINATION 1

(Masquenada)

Stand in a modified first position parallel, as in the preceding exercise, with the arms neutral. As mentioned at the beginning of the chapter, "Masquenada" is the name of a piece of music played by trumpeter Hugh Masekela. The theme originated from the African-based music of Brazil, and Masekela, a black South African, brings a traditional African flavor to the music. The music is available on the album, "All-Time Hits of Hugh Masekela" (GAS 116, MGM) or on "Americanization of Ooga Booga" (MGM S-4371), an older album.

Count and   Hop on the left foot and lift the right foot slightly off the floor. At the same time cross the arms at the wrist at waist level in front of the body, with the elbows bent and the lower arms parallel to the floor. (See the illustration.)

1   Place the right heel against the floor, turning the front of the foot first to the left, then to the right, while lifting the entire left foot slightly off the floor. At the same time begin to open the arms from the wrist, with the palms flat and toward the ceiling, and move the hips forward.

and   Place the ball of the right foot on the floor, keeping the left foot slightly lifted, and continue to open the arms. (See the illustration.)

2   Place the right heel on the floor, continue to open the arms, and move the hip to the right.

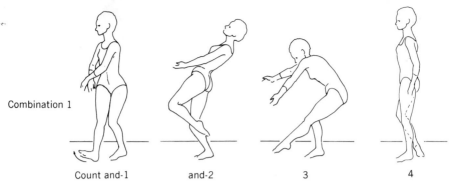

Combination 1

Count and-1   and-2   3   4

3   Step about six inches backward with the right foot and lift
     the left foot slightly off the floor in front, at the same time
     leaning the torso forward. Continue to open the arms, and
     move the hip backward. (See the illustration.)

4   Place the left foot on the floor in front, bring both arms
     down at the sides with the palm toward the thigh, and
     move the hip back to center. When stepping with the left
     foot, let the right foot pivot so that the heel is up and the
     toe points to the right. (See the illustration.)

     Repeat three times.

Note: The movement of the arms and hip should be very smooth and
continuous. Each four counts should take the student forward a few
inches, even though the knees remain bent and the feet leave the floor
only slightly.

Do the same movement but emphasize the forward push through the
hip on count 1, so that the body travels forward. When the basic movement is familiar, do it at half time (twice as slow).

COMBINATION 2

(Masquenada Turn)

Stand in a modified first position parallel, with the feet comfortably
apart (no more than four inches) and slightly turned out, and with the
arms in neutral. Plié slightly in both knees.

Count and   Repeat the foot movement of the first "and" count of the
             preceding exercise—hop on the left foot and lift the right
             foot slightly off the floor—but keep the arms neutral.

1   Repeat the foot movement of count 1 of the preceding
             exercise—place the right heel against the floor, turning the
             front of the foot first to the left, then to the right, while
             lifting the enitre left foot slightly off the floor and while
             moving the hip forward—but keep the arms neutral.

2   Cross the left foot over the right, placing the ball of the left foot about twelve inches to the right, and immediately place the ball of the right foot on the floor. At the same time cross the arms at the wrist slightly in front of the hip, with the palms toward the hip.

and   Pivot all the way around to the right on the balls of both feet. The right heel must be lifted slightly away from the floor.

a   Lift the right foot slightly off the floor.

3   Return the right foot to the floor in the same place.

and   Lift the left foot slightly off the floor.

4   Return the left foot to the floor in the same place.

Repeat three times.

Note: The direction of movement for the first "and" count and for count 1 is forward, although the actual forward distance covered is slight. Count 2 should be performed sharply, with the elbows bending slightly to accent the count.

Do the same movement but emphasize the forward push through the hip on count 1, pushing the hip forward as far as possible and deepening the plié. Repeat three times.

COMBINATION 3

(Masquenada Bend and Turn)

Stand in a modified first position parallel as for the previous exercise. Plié slightly in both knees.

Count and   Repeat the first "and" count of Combination 1: Hop on the left foot and lift the right foot slightly off the floor. At the same time cross the arms at the wrist at waist level in front of the body, with the elbows bent and the lower arms parallel to the floor.

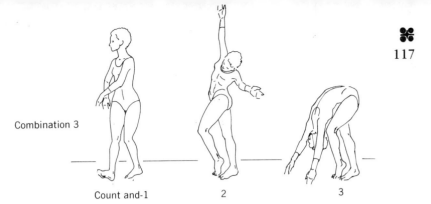

Combination 3

Count and-1   2   3

1   Repeat count 1 of Combination 1 except for the hip movement: Place the right heel against the floor, turning the front of the foot first to the left, then to the right, while lifting the entire left foot slightly off the floor. At the same time begin to open the arms from the wrist, with the palms flat and toward the ceiling. (See the illustration.)

2   Cross the left foot over the right, placing the ball of the left foot about twelve inches to the right. Straighten the right knee and shift the body weight primarily to the right leg. Lift the upper body and then move it to the left side as far as possible, facing front and bending at the waist. While bending, reach forward with both arms, holding the left arm slightly below the head and the right above, with the elbows and fingers straight and the palms toward each other. (See the illustration.)

3   Begin to lower the upper body and arms as a single unit, first turning from the left side toward the floor and then moving directly toward the floor. Continue lowering the upper body until the head almost touches the left knee and the arms touch the floor. (See the illustration.) Then pivot to the right on the balls of both feet.

4   Complete the turn by gradually lifting the upper body while the arms remain at the sides in neutral position. During the turn the upper body follows the lower body, and the upper body makes a complete circle by itself.

Repeat on the opposite side, and then repeat again on both sides.

COMBINATION 4

(Along Comes Mary)

Stand in first position parallel with the arms neutral. The five parts of this combination are meant to go with "Along Comes Mary" as played by Hugh Masekela on "Next Album" (MGM S-4415) or on "All-Time

Hits of Hugh Masekela" (GAS 116, MGM) so that the fourth part synchronizes with his trumpet solo.

Part 1

Count 1   Cross the right leg behind the left leg diagonally backward and to the left about twenty-four inches. Bend the left knee and focus the head diagonally left. At the same time reach both arms diagonally to the left, with the right arm crossing the body below the waist and with both elbows straight. Do all of this movement simultaneously and very sharply.

2-4   Hold.

Count 1   Contract through the center of the body to move the hip forward, and bring the right leg forward and diagonally to the right, with the knee bent and the ball of the foot touching the floor. Move the arms to either side of the body, with the elbows bent and close to the waist, and hold the lower arms horizontal while the palms are flat and toward the ceiling. Do all this movement smoothly and easily.

2-4   Hold.

Repeat all of the counts above on the left side.

Part 2

Count 1   Step to the right with the right foot to move in as large a circle as possible. At the same time bend the upper body forward from the waist until the back is almost parallel to the floor, and hold the arms directly to the sides with the palms toward the floor.

2   Step in a circle to the right with the left foot.

3   Step to the right with the right foot to complete the circle.

4   Bring the left foot to place next to the right and straighten the upper body to center while moving the arms to neutral position, to stand in an easy first position parallel.

Part 3

Count and   Plié in both knees and bend the arms at the elbow so that the lower arms are directed upward and the palms are directed away from the body at about shoulder level.

1   Jump to the right, bending the upper body to the right and landing in a plié on the right foot, with the left leg extended (the knee straight) diagonally to the left. At the same time continue to lift the arms so that the elbows straighten.

2   Bend the left knee, cross it in back of the right knee, and step on the left foot. At the same time begin to stretch the arms outward, away from the center of the body.

3   Step about twelve inches to the right with the right foot and begin to lower the outstretched arms to the sides.

4   Bring the left foot to place next to the right and continue to lower the arms until they reach neutral.

1-4   Repeat to the left side.

Repeat the jump and the other movements six more times (twenty-four more counts), alternating right and left and ending with a movement to the left.

Count 1-4   Step in a circle to the right (stepping with the right foot, the left foot, and the right foot, and then bringing the left foot next to the right), and move the arms upward with bent elbows and then downward with straight elbows, as in the earlier counts.

Count 1-4   Step in a circle to the left, starting on the left foot, and move the arms upward and then downward as before.

Part 4 (Sweep Step)

Count 1   Step about twelve inches to the right with the right foot and plié to shift the weight to the right foot. Extend the right hip at the same time (the left foot lifts from the floor

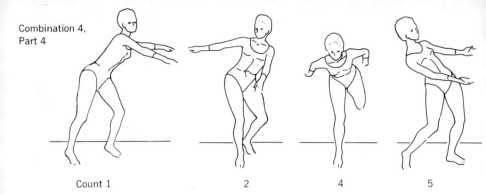

Combination 4,
Part 4

Count 1   2   4   5

except for the big toe). Extend the arms diagonally to the left and downward with the palms toward the back and the right arm a little lower than the left. (See the illustration.)

2   Begin to bring the left foot in toward the right and extend the right hip farther to the right. At the same time, begin to bring the arms toward center. (See the illustration.)

3   Continue to bring the left foot toward the right, the right hip farther to the right, and the arms toward center.

4   Sweep the left foot in next to the right and then backward off the floor, ending with the left knee bent and directed to the floor. Move the hip backward and to the left, and move the arms past center to the right side. Let the sweeping of the left foot cause the upper body to lean forward, with a diagonal line from the head to the hip. (See the illustration.)

5   Step to the left with the left foot, placing the foot about five inches to the left of its position in count 1, and shift the weight from the right foot to the left. At the same time move the arms to the left in front of the hip and close to the body, with the elbows slightly bent. (See the illustration.)

6   Place the right foot next to the left and shift the weight to divide it evenly between the feet. Continue the motion of the arms, changing the direction toward center and forward.

7   Continue moving the arms toward center and forward, lifting them until they are directly overhead and centered.

8   Bring both arms down to neutral, leading with the elbows.

Note: This part of the combination is done to a slow count of eight, following the solo line of the trumpet.

Part 5 (Steps in a Square)

Count and   Move both arms up, extending the left arm directly to the left side and the right arm across the chest.

Start

Facing

Facing

Facing

Facing

Facing

1　Step to the left with the left foot, with a plié in both knees, while facing forward. (See the illustration.)

2　Step to the left with the right foot to place it next to the left foot. Continue to face forward.

3　Step to the left with the left foot.

and　Move the arms to the other side, extending the right arm directly to the right side and the left arm across the chest, and take a quarter turn to the right.

1　Step to the right with the right foot, moving along the second side of a square and facing the center of the square.

2　Step to the right with the left foot to place it next to the right foot.

3　Step to the right with the right foot.

and　Move the arms to the other side – to the left – and take a quarter turn to the right to face opposite the direction faced on the first three counts.

1　Step to the left with the left foot, moving along the third side of the square and facing away from the center of the square.

2　Step to the left with the right foot to place it next to the left foot.

3　Step to the left with the left foot.

and　Move the arms to the other side – to the right – and take a quarter turn to the right.

1　Step to the right with the right foot, moving along the fourth side of the square and facing the center of the square.

2　Step to the right with the left foot to place it next to the right foot.

3　Step to the right with the right foot to complete the square.

and   Bring the arms to neutral and take a quarter turn to the right to face in the original direction, away from the square.

Repeat all five parts of the combination.

Do the "Along Comes Mary" combination in two groups, with the second group starting one beat (count) after the first group to cause a call-and-response effect between the groups. When the first group does the jumps (the first thirty-two counts of part 3), the second group advances a count so that the jumps are done by both groups at the same time. After the jumps, the second group waits a count and then stays a count behind until the jumps are done again.

COMbiNATION 5

(Grazing in the Grass)

Stand in first position parallel with the arms neutral, and plié in both knees. The three parts of this combination are meant to be accompanied by "Grazing in the Grass" as played by Hugh Masekela on the albums "The Best of Hugh Masekela" (UNI 7305-1) and "Promise of a Future" (UNI 73028). The latter is a two-record set.

Part 1

Count 1   Step directly forward about eight to ten inches with the right foot, and maintain the plié. At the same time, begin to lift the arms forward with the palms up and the elbows straight.

and   Deepen the plié on the right side, and continue to lift the arms.

2   Step directly forward about eight to ten inches with the left foot, and maintain the plié. Continue to lift the arms.

and   Deepen the plié on the left side, and continue to lift the arms.

3   Step directly forward with the right foot, as in count 1, and continue to lift the arms.

and Deepen the plié on the right side, and complete the lifting of the arms.

4 Contract the hips forward to center, lower the head, and bring the ball of the left foot into place next to the right foot. At the same time, bring the arms down to the sides and clench the hands into fists.

Part 2 (in double time, twice as fast)

Count 1 Step to the right side about six inches with the right foot. At the same time begin to lift the arms at the sides but slightly forward, keeping the elbows straight and unclenching the hands.

2 Bring the left foot in next to the right foot, and lift the arms until they are straight overhead. Then bend the elbows and start to bring them straight down while starting to move the forearms toward each other in front of the body.

3 Step to the right side about six inches with the right foot. At the same time, continue to lower the arms until the wrists cross at about the level of the chest.

Repeat the three counts on the left side.

Part 3 (same tempo as part 2)

Count and Round the back and plié deeply in both knees.

1 Take a small jump to the right, landing with the right foot first and then the left.

and Clap the hands at about chest level with the elbows bent and the hands a few inches in front of the chest.

a Clap the hands again at chest level.

2 Take a small jump to the left, landing with the left foot first and then the right.

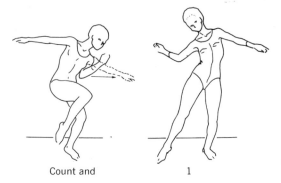

Combination 6, Part 1

Count and   1

and   Clap the hands at chest level, as before.

a   Clap the hands again at chest level.

3   Step to the right with the right foot.

and   Bring the left foot in close to the right foot, stepping on the ball of the left foot, and at the same time clap the hands.

4   Step to the left with the left foot.

and   Bring the right foot in close to the left foot, stepping on the ball of the right foot, and at the same time clap the hands.

Repeat all three parts of the combination.

COMBINATION 6

(Cold Sweat)

Stand in first position parallel with the feet easy (comfortably apart and open rather than carefully positioned) and with the arms in second position (extended directly to the sides). The first four counts of this combination are the same as the four counts of Plié Exercise 4 in Chapter 3. The entire sequence is designed for "Cold Sweat" as played by Mongo Santamaria, available on "Heavy Sounds" (Columbia CS 99-70), "Mongo Santamaria's Greatest Hits" (Columbia CS-1060), and "Soul Bag" (Columbia CS-9653).

Part 1

Count and   Plié in the left knee and bring the right knee diagonally across the left thigh. At the same time bend the left elbow and bring it in toward the center of the body. This causes the upper body to tilt slightly to the left. (See the illustration.)

1   Stretch the right leg directly to the right side with the toe toward the floor, and straighten the left knee slightly. At the same time return the left arm to second position and bend the right elbow down a little, rotating the hand so

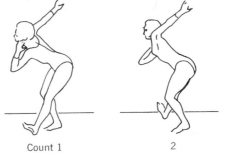

Combination 6, Part 3

Count 1   2

that the palm is forward, as the upper body tilts slightly to the right. (See the illustration.)

and   Repeat the movements of the first "and" count, starting from the position at the end of count 1. (Return the right arm to second position as a part of the movement.)

2   Repeat count 1.

and   Repeat the first "and" count, returning the right arm to second position as a part of the movement.

3-4   Continue to repeat the movements.

Part 2

Count 1   Step directly forward with the right foot and extend the right hip sideward during the step. At the same time, move the arms low and close to the hips with the palms toward the hips. The arms move in simple opposition: when the right foot moves forward, the left arm swings forward.

2   Step directly forward with the left foot, extend the left hip sideward during the step, and swing the right arm forward, keeping it low and close to the hip.

3   Step directly forward with the right foot, extend the right hip sideward, and swing the left arm forward.

4   Step directly forward with the left foot, extend the left hip sideward, and swing the right arm forward.

Part 3

Count 1   Step directly backward with the right foot and lift the ball of the left foot off the floor. At the same time tilt the upper body slightly forward, extend the hips directly backward, and move the arms: the right arm is extended to the side and slightly backward above shoulder level while the left elbow is bent down and slightly in toward the center of the body. (See the illustration.)

2   Step directly backward with the left foot, lift the ball of the right foot off the floor, extend the left arm to the side and slightly backward above shoulder level, and bend the right elbow down and slightly in toward the center of the body. (See the illustration.)

3-8   Repeat the steps directly backward.

Part 4 (Catch Step)

and   Turn diagonally to the right, bend the right knee, and lift it until the foot is about five inches off the floor, and begin a step backward with the right foot.

a   Step with the right foot about eighteen inches behind the left foot, and immediately lift the left foot slightly off the floor. At the same time, bring the left arm in from its extended position on the last count of part 3 of the combination, and lower the arms toward neutral.

1   Step in place with the left foot and complete the movement of the arms to neutral.

2   Step forward on the right foot, bring the upper body and head back to center from the tilted position of part 3, and swing the left arm forward in simple opposition to the movement of the right leg.

3   Step forward with the left foot and swing the right arm forward.

4   Step forward with the right foot and swing the left arm forward.

5   Step forward with the left foot and swing the right arm forward.

6   Extend the right leg straight up toward the ceiling as far as possible, extend the right arm to the right side and the left arm forward. The right leg and both arms should be fully extended.

7   Step in place with the right foot and return the arms to neutral.

and   Step in place with the left foot.

8   Step in place with the right foot.

and   Turn slightly to the left to face front again.

Note: The steps of the first four counts of this catch step are the same as the steps of Catch Step Exercise 1 in Chapter 3. (The arm and body movements are *not* the same as those described in Catch Step Exercise 2 and Catch Step Exercise 3 in that chapter.)

Repeat all four parts of the combination on the other side, starting with a lift of the left leg.

7

class planning, improvisation, and composition

The most important consideration in class planning is not any single area or way of organizing, but the class as a whole and how it works as an entire experience. The teacher should look upon the class as a working unit with many parts, rather than as a series of separate exercises. In choosing areas to cover and ways to present material, the teacher should consider the interrelations of the parts and how all of them relate to the skills and potentials of the students.

Because this book has been divided into areas of movement, the teacher must choose from several chapters to develop a unified dance experience. In addition, the teacher may choose methods of improvisation or composition described in this chapter. The teacher's choices should aid the students in gaining a sense of individual expression in jazz dance, along with competence in a variety of movements.

planning the areas of exercise

In choosing exercises for a class, the teacher is almost always bound by fixed periods of time. Classes at a college level usually run from one hour to a little more than an hour and a half. At the high school level, though, classes typically meet in periods of twenty to fifty minutes. How the teacher allots time is thus a serious concern.

The beginning of a class should always be a warm-up. There are, of course, many ways to handle a warm-up, and these ways determine to what extent the body is ready to move. The second area of exercise to introduce during a class is that of rhythmic exercises. The third area is technique (isolations and turns). In some classes, the teacher may find it beneficial to have technique precede rhythmic exercises. In any class, the two areas should be chosen to relate either to the fourth or the fifth area in the period. The fourth area of exercise is movement across the floor. The fifth is movement sequences or combinations.

Area of Exercise	One-Hour Class	One-and-a-Half-Hour Class
1. Warm-up exercises	10 minutes	10 minutes
2. Rhythmic exercises	10 minutes	15 minutes
3. Technique (isolations and turns)	15 minutes	25 minutes
4. Movement across the floor	10 minutes	15 minutes
5. Sequences or combinations	15 minutes	25 minutes

    The order and the listed lengths of time of these areas are suggestions only. There will be many exceptions. There will be classes, for instance, in which more time needs to be spent on rhythm than on any other area. The teacher should always be sensitive to what is needed by a group of students, and when. Suggested times for two common class periods are shown here.

    The division of each class period into specific movement areas and specific time periods may seem routine to students, even when the time periods are varied depending on the needs of the class. The teacher may need to achieve greater variety and interest by changing the music often and by challenging the students with increasingly difficult movements or tempos, provided the students are ready for them. (The use and selection of music is described in detail in the next chapter.)

plANNiNG THE USE OF SPACE

    The essential requirement for teaching is to know the subject matter. If the teacher is familiar with the subject, there are only a few techniques that need to be considered. One of them is the arrangement of students in space.

    The teacher should have students positioned so that each one can be seen easily for some part of the time. Generally, this means that students who work in the front line one day should move back a row on the following day so that other students may come to the front, or some alternative change of place should be used.

    In movement across the floor, the arrangement of students also should be changed to permit every student to be observed closely from time to time. Once lines or groups of students are ready for a movement across the floor, each line or group must be given a cue as to when to begin. The cue may be as simple as, "Ready, and." The counts between each group should be indicated: eight counts, sixteen, etc. The students also must be given a way to return to place after the movement. An efficient way is to have each group break in the middle once the group has completed the movement across the floor, with the students on either end leading a file back to the starting position.

When a sequence of movement is being introduced, the teacher should present it to the class as a whole and then supervise practice by a half or a fourth of the class at a time.

In any arrangement of students, the more capable ones should be spread out so that the students who have problems are able to see them and use them as models. Similarly, the more capable students may help with demonstrations and assist in other ways, freeing the teacher to work with the students who need help most. The teacher may find it useful to take these students to a separate area, where they can concentrate on their weaknesses.

Discussions of the ideal class size are fascinating but seldom practical. The problem almost always is going to be what to do with large classes; small ones are rare in most schools. The teacher who has a very large class must take care to arrange the students to provide enough moving space and a clear sight of any person who demonstrates to the class. The teacher also must be sensitive and skillful to manage the class effectively. Techniques only come alive through the personality, knowledge, and involvement of the teacher, and the teacher's ability to communicate these to others.

pRiNciplEs of impRovisATioN

In the beginning stages of jazz dance there is little room for improvisation. During these stages students should be limited to improvisation of the theme-and-variation sort. The reason is that jazz dance requires the ability to move with particular qualities along particular stylistic lines and with special rhythmic emphasis. To spend much time on open-ended, do-as-you-feel sessions will not help students to gain this ability, which is the basis for advanced improvisation. In their beginning experiences with jazz dance, then, students must learn to keep time and to work in specific ways.

However, the teacher must never lose sight of the students' eventual need to express their own emotions in jazz dance. This expression is difficult in dance of any kind. It is talked about too much and done too little. Modern dance has long been concerned with the expression of emotion through movement, but as time has gone on and modern dance has become a dominant art form, widely taught and widely performed, the externalization of the dance style associated with a given emotion has often become more important than the emotion itself. The same danger exists for jazz dance. Students of jazz dance must develop technique and be able to handle their instruments smoothly, sharply, and rhythmically. But more important, they must eventually be able to become emotionally involved in what they do. Each student must bring himself—his life's experiences and emotions—to the movement.

For most black students, who have been in touch with the sources of jazz dance all their lives, emotional involvement and its projection are not difficult. However, for many white students, the involvement and projection must be developed. How does a teacher aid this development? Improvisation is only part of the answer. It offers an opportunity for the projection of emotions, but the emotions must be felt in the first place. To encourage emotional involvement, the teacher should help students to associate musical qualities with the feelings that humans experience everyday. The teacher may suggest that students discover their emotional associations with music through the lyrics of songs, through descriptions on the backs of record albums, or by listening to the music in a concentrated fashion and taking time to think about their reactions.

five designs for improvisation

More advanced students may follow a number of designs for improvisation, including the five described here. First, the students may move to a particular piece of music as the music brings forth movement in them. If a student is clearly in tune with the music, he and the music become one. It takes a sensitive and experienced teacher to tell when the student is doing this, when his personal expression and the selection of music merge, when he truly is with it. This improvisational design may be set up in several ways. For relatively inexperienced students, the teacher may have all the members of the class participate in the improvisation at the same time. After the students feel at ease with the experience, the teacher may change the music every minute or two so that the students must change their improvisation to stay with the music. Or the teacher may have some members of the class dance while the rest watch. For instance, half of the students may form a circle and dance while the other students sit in a large circle around the dancers. After a time, the two groups change places and activities: the students in the outer circle get up, form a smaller circle, and improvise, while the others take their places in the outer circle and watch.

The second design for improvisation starts with all but two or three students sitting in a large circle. Those two or three improvise — not necessarily in communion with the music — until each one feels that he has exhausted his creative energies. Then he selects one of the sitting students to take his place, and that student improvises for a time and then selects another student, etc., until every class member has danced. This design allows the students to work under a kind of performance pressure, creating as they perform.

The third design moves back and forth between structured and improvised movement. The teacher begins by setting a position for count 1, with no instructions given for the following seven counts but with a different position set for the next count 1, the count 1 after that, and so on. The students must improvise from one set position to another, moving through each set position as they go.

The fourth improvisational design is similar to the third. The teacher has the students work in pairs. One student takes eight counts to dance from one set position to another, improvising in between, as in the third design. At the same time the second student performs structured movement in a slow and sustained fashion, moving directly and deliberately from one set position to the next, with no improvisation whatsoever. The second student goes through the same set position on successive counts of 1 as the first student. Both students begin and end at the same time. After a few repetitions of the design, the teacher has the students reverse their roles.

In the fifth design, students associate movement with the music of particular instruments. For instance, the teacher may have three students work with music played by a trio. (Or more students may join in if several of them identify with one instrument.) One student improvises to the bass line, another to the piano, and another to the drum. The students do not necessarily try to dance in direct correspondence to the sound of each instrument. Rather, they may try to dance the effect of the instrument — what they feel the artist is saying through it. When the instruments come together in the chorus or preceding and following solos, the students may continue to improvise or they may dance to choreography chosen previously.

Let me stress again that most of these improvisational designs are meant for the more advanced students. Beginning students must work to develop special techniques in jazz dance as a priority, and therefore they need to stay with basic concerns. Only after the students have some competence in the basics should they go on to the more experimental improvisational designs.

pRinciplEs of composiTion

Ways of approaching composition in modern jazz dance are as varied as the music available. There is one important prerequisite, however: students must be able to move well before they can carry out successful composition. Students need a good sense of rhythm, the ability to syncopate, the ability to isolate body parts, etc. In brief, they must feel at home in the movements, qualities, and feelings of jazz dance before they can create jazz dance compositions.

Feelings are more important than qualities or movements in the creation of jazz dance. If the expression of feelings is not given priority, then composition becomes an entanglement of rules of form, just as movement without feeling becomes an entanglement of rules of technique. When a student uses only three square feet of a large performance area, the critical consideration is not some "rule" about the use of stage space. Rather, the key question is how well the student has communicated feeling in that space.

foUR AppROAchEs TO composiTion

The compositional approaches that follow are given in order of difficulty. Each has been used successfully by students with competence in jazz dance movement. Of course, many other approaches are possible.

In the call-and-response approach, one movement phrase represents the call and an answering phrase — suggested by the call — is the response. The form is basic in jazz music and is found in early worksongs, field hollers, ring shouts, and gospel and spiritual music. Recordings by Aretha Franklin, Ray Charles, Marvin Gaye, Tammi Terrell, etc., include a call and response between the featured singer and the group. Any music that includes a call and response may work well for a dance composition that uses the same form.

Students may compose movement for both the call and response or for the call alone with no movement during the response or for the response alone. When two students or groups of students are available to dance, the composition may have one dance the call and the other the response. Or the composition may follow the pattern of some early worksongs: one dancer or group does the call, the other the response, and then both dance together. Or the composition may follow another worksong pattern: call, response, both together, and then the response continuing while the call enters now and again. These patterns occur in many gospel songs as well as jazz pieces, and it is not essential that traditional worksongs be used.

The approach to composition based on improvisation may follow any of the designs described earlier. Perhaps the most rewarding type of improvisational approach follows the third design, moving back and forth between structured and improvised movement. The teacher gives the students a position on count 1 and other positions on succeeding counts of 1. Using eight counts to a measure, the students improvise from one set position to the next. At first, the teacher should encourage the students to improvise for each of the seven counts between set positions and to do eight or more measures, depending on the students' inventiveness. Some of the improvisations may be repeated as the structure of a dance composition.

More advanced students may try an improvisational approach that follows design four, in which the students work in pairs. One student improvises from set position to set position, as described above, while the other takes time to move slowly from one set position to the next, with no improvisation. The two students meet on successive counts of 1, even though the first student probably is moving much faster. After the students have done this several times, the teacher may have them reverse roles. For advanced students, the teacher may reduce the counts to six or four.

The third approach to composition relates movement to the music of particular instruments. (This approach is similar to the fifth design for improvisation, and such an improvisation might become the basis for a composition, but the approach does not need to rely on improvisation.) The students may compose a dance for three dancers or for three groups of dancers to the music of a trio, with the movement for each corresponding to the feeling of one of the instruments. In the chorus and riffs — when the instruments come together — the dancers' movements also may come together. Or one dancer may move to the music of the solos while a group moves to the choruses and riffs.

As variations on this approach, the students may do compositions to the music of a quartet or quintet, or to the sections of a band so that one dancer or group of dancers follows the brass, another the rhythm section, etc. Like other approaches to composition, this one has many alternatives.

The fourth approach to composition focuses on historical subject matter. Students who try this approach should have a clear understanding of the development of jazz music and musicians in the United States. For instance, "Three Aspects of John Coltrane" could be the title of a dance composition that reflects the evolution of John Coltrane as an artist. Such a composition might take three pieces of music representing the three periods of development in his music, and the student who undertook the composition would need to select the pieces carefully and put them or parts of them together on a tape to choreograph a dance to them.

Similarly, a student might compose "A Tribute to Lady Day" based on research into the life and work of Billie Holiday, and the music could be a collage of her songs on tape, Or a student might select any one of hundreds of jazz artists.

More advanced students could approach composition by taking historical subject matter that does not relate directly to music but that concerns the sources of jazz. This area includes the entire realm of black experience in the United States.

8

MUSIC

Many sources of music are useful in jazz dance classes. Clapping, hand drums, live musicians, and recordings all can be helpful. As with the other aspects of jazz dance, the most important consideration in selecting and using music is the class as a whole. The teacher should think of music as a part of the over-all class experience.

At times, music is a valuable stimulus to improvisation and composition, but in a typical class music is used to accompany exercises. Both live and recorded music can serve this purpose.

plANNiNq thE usE of Music

In the early parts of a class, when basic warm-up and technique exercises are done, a hand drum is usually more efficient than recorded music. It is certainly easier to talk during the movement and to have students stop and then continue if a hand drum is employed. Recorded music is worthwhile in the early parts of a class only when it is possible to go through an entire movement without having to interrupt the class to change the music. (I have seen a class in which a teacher had to locate a given spot on a given band of a record to do a technique that only took thirty seconds.)

Variety in music is desirable – it helps to create and maintain student interest – and recorded music offers variety. The most effective accompaniment may be an intermixture of records and a hand drum.

Live accompaniment is available in some teaching situations. A trap drummer or a pianist or both of these with a bassist can be quite suitable for a jazz dance class *provided the musicians are truly jazz musicians.* The teacher who is not familiar with jazz music may select musicians or records that offer bland copies of the music respected by the best jazz artists. There is an immense difference between Ray Charles and Elvis Presley even though they sing some of the same songs. Both jazz dance and jazz music are expressions of black experience, and the teacher who approaches jazz dance seriously should strive to select true jazz music. One valuable use of the music is to reflect the true culture of the dance.

selecting music

The teacher who is already familiar with jazz music will find it easy to make selections of records suitable for jazz dance. The teacher's only concern will be to stay in touch with the records that are currently popular. Perhaps the best way to do this is to listen to one of the radio stations that play black music. There is at least one in every major city in the United States, and the experience of listening will help the teacher know new jazz artists as well as the specific records that are likely to be popular with students.

Another source of information about records are charts of best-selling single 45 records and albums. These charts are published in most newspapers and in several show business magazines. Many of the single records listed appear on the charts for two weeks or so and then disappear. The records that achieve a listing may or may not qualify as the "real thing" for the accompaniment of jazz dance, and the teacher should be selective about these records. Some charts show national popularity and others give local or regional preferences.

The teacher who is not familiar with jazz music may begin with the recommended albums and the recommended recording artists listed later in this chapter. The teacher should also listen to one of the radio stations that play black music and should take some time to look at the albums in record stores as well as the listings in record catalogs. The teacher may be baffled by the many categories of albums in record stores. As indicated in Chapter 1, classifications of jazz music or dance often lead to erroneous conclusions. Black music that record stores classify as blues, folk, gospel, rhythm and blues, jazz, and (to some extent) popular all has the same general characteristics and the same source. The division of black music into distinct categories is a superficial division, and the teacher should not hesitate to use the music of any category when it is suitable to jazz dance. (In the listing of recommended recording artists, I have included only one singer of gospel music — Mahalia Jackson — and none of the singers of prison songs and other folk songs such as Rev. Gary Davis and Sonny Terry. Gospel music such as that recorded by the Staple Singers and prison songs are perfectly suitable for jazz dance, but the singing distracts many dance teachers. For the same reason I have listed relatively few of the popular rhythm and blues groups.)

Clerks in record stores usually will provide valuable help in locating a particular record or records by a particular artist. Another source of help is the *Schwann Supplementary Catalog,* which is issued twice a year and is available in most record stores. The Schwann company also publishes a monthly guide to records which gives new listings and also records that have been issued in the past two years or so; the *Supplementary Catalog* gives older listings. Both Schwann publications divide black music into two main groups: popular and jazz. Again the division is superficial and, of course, not all the records listed in either category have a strong relation to the traditions of black culture.

RECOMMENDEd AlbUMS

The list here is a personal one. It includes records that I have used again and again. Many other albums might be included, but these are the ones I prefer and that I would most recommend to the teacher who is unfamiliar with jazz music. (The teacher should also note the records by Hugh Masekela and Mongo Santamaria listed at the beginning of Chapter 6.)

I have retained the Schwann division of popular and jazz albums not because the division is very meaningful but because it may aid in locating the records. (See note, page xii.)

Popular

> Brown, James
> > It's a Mother (King S-1063)
> > Popcorn (King S-1055)
>
> Fifth Dimension
> > Age of Aquarius (Soul City 92005)

Franklin, Aretha
Runnin' Out of Fools (Columbia CS-9081)

Gaye, Marvin
With Tammi Terrell (Tamla S-277)

Impressions
This Is My Country (Curtom 8001)

Makeba, Miriam
Makeba! (Reprise S-6310)
Many Voices (Kapp 3274)
Voices of Africa (RCA Victor LSP-2845)

Masekela, Hugh
Emancipation (UNI 73007)
Exciting Sounds of Africa and Its People (UNI 73020)
Promise of a Future (2 vols.) (UNI 73028)

Redding, Otis
Sings Soul (Atco S-33-284)

Temptations
Cloud Nine (Gordy S-939)

Watts 103rd St. Rhythm Band
Watts 103rd St. Rhythm Band (Warner Bros./7 Arts S-1741)

Wonder, Stevie
Down to Earth (Tamla S-272)
For Once in My Life (Tamla S-291)

Jazz

Big Black
Message to Our Ancestors (UNI 73012)

Blakey, Art
Soul Finger (Lime 86018)

Bobo, Willie
Bobo Motion (Verve 68699)
Evil Ways (Verve 68781)
Juicy (Verve 68685)

Charles, Ray
    Genius + Soul = Jazz (Impulse S-2)

Coltrane, John
    Kulu Sé Mama (Impulse S-9106)
    Love Supreme (Impulse S-77)
    My Favorite Things (Atlantic S-1361)

Davis, Miles
    Milestones (Columbia CS-9428)
    Sketches of Spain (Columbia CS-8271)

Ellington, Duke
    With Coltrane (Impulse S-30)

Freedom Sounds
    People Get Ready (Atlantic S-1492)

Gillespie, Dizzy
    My Way (Solid State 18054)

Green, Grant
    Goin' West (Blue Note 84310)
    His Majesty, King Funk (Verve 68627)

Hancock, Herbie
    Inventions & Dimensions (Blue Note 84147)

Handy, John
    New View (Columbia CS-9497)

Jackson, Milt
    Bags & Brass (Riverside S-3021)

Jazz Crusaders
    Talk That Talk (Pacific Jazz 20106)
    Tough Talk (Pacific Jazz S-58)

Kirk, Roland
    Here Comes the Whistleman (Atlantic S-3007)
    I Talk with Spirits (Limelight 86008)

Lateef, Yusef
Complete (Atlantic S-1499)
Jazz Round the World (Impulse S-56)

Lewis, Ramsey
Maiden Voyage (Cadet S-811)
Mother Nature's Son (Cadet S-821)

McCann, Les
Bucket of Grease (Limelight 86043)
Gospel Truth (Pacific Jazz S-69)

Mingus, Charlie
Blues & Roots (Atlantic S-1305)
Mingus Ah Um (Columbia CS-8171)

Monk, Thelonious
Greatest Hits (Columbia CS-9775)
Music (with Coltrane) (Riverside S-3004)

Montgomery, Wes
California Dreaming (Verve 68672)
Down Here on the Ground (A&M 3006)

Moody, James
Blues & Other Colors (Milestone 9023)

Peterson, Oscar
Soul Español (Limelight 86044)
West Side Story (Verve 68454)

Roach, Max
Drums Unlimited (Atlantic S-1467)

Sanders, Pharaoh
Karma (Impulse S-9181)
Tauhid (Impulse S-9138)

Santamaria, Mongo
Drums & Chants (Tico 1149)
Stone Soul (Columbia CS-9780)

Shepp, Archie
Fire Music (Impulse S-86)

Silver, Horace
Horace-Scope (Blue Note 84042)
Song for My Father (Blue Note 84185)

Smith, Jimmy
Dynamic Duo (with Wes Montgomery) (Verve 68678)

Turrentine, Stanley
Rough 'n Tumble (Blue Note 84240)
Soul (Sunset 5255)

Wilson, Gerald
California Soul (Pacific Jazz 20135)
Moment of Truth (Pacific Jazz S-61)

RECOMMENdEd RECORdiNG ARTiSTS

The artists listed under the heading "popular" include those whose recordings were put out as albums after the artists' success with single 45 records. These artists combine singing and playing. Most of the "jazz" artists are instrumentalists only. The division is less important than the fact that all of the artists listed offer musical expressions in the tradition of the culture that produced jazz dance, a culture in which music and dance started together.

Popular

Booker T. and the M.G.'s
Brown, James
Butler, Jerry
Cooke, Sam
Fifth Dimension
Four Tops
Franklin, Aretha
Gaye, Marvin

Impressions
Isley Bros.
Jackson, Chuck
Martha and the Vandellas
Miracles
Redding, Otis
Robinson, Smokey and the
    Miracles

Ruffin, Jimmy
Sam and Dave
Shirelles
Shirley, Don
Sly and the Family Stone
Temptations
Terrell, Tammi
Tex, Joe

Thomas, Carla
Turner, Ike and Tina
Walker, Jr., and the All Stars
Watts 103rd St. Rhythm Band
Wells, Mary
Wilson, Jackie
Wonder, Stevie
Young-Holt Unlimited

Jazz

Adderley, Julian "Cannonball"
Adderley, Nat
Afro-Blues Quintet Plus One
Almeida, Laurinda
Ammons, Gene
Armstrong, Louis
Baker, LaVern
Basie, Count
Big Black
Big Maybelle
Blakey, Art
Bobo, Willie
Brown, Charles
Brown, Clifford
Bryant, Ray
Burrell, Kenny
Byard, Jaki
Byrd, Donald
Carter, Benny
Charles, Ray

Clark, Sonny
Clarke, Kenny
Cobb, Arnett
Cole, Cozy
Coleman, Ornette
Coltrane, John
Crawford, Hank
Curtis, King
Davis, Eddie "Lockjaw"
Davis, Miles
Davison, "Wild Bill"
Dodds, Baby
Dolphy, Eric
Donaldson, Lou
Dorham, Kenny
Ellington, Duke
Ervin, Booker
Farmer, Art
Flanagan, Tommy
Forrest, Jimmy

Freedom Sounds
Fuller, Curtis
Garner, Erroll
Gillespie, Dizzy
Gray, Wardell
Green, Bennie
Green, Grant
Griffin, Johnny
Gryce, Gigi
Hamilton, Chico
Hampton, Lionel
Hampton, Slide
Hancock, Herbie
Handy, John
Harris, Eddie
Hawes, Hampton
Hawkins, Coleman
Henderson, Fletcher
Henderson, Joe
Hill, Andrew
Hines, Earl
Hodges, Johnny
Holiday, Billie
Holmes, Richard
Hope, Elmo
Hubbard, Freddie
Hug, Armand
Humes, Helen
Hutcherson, Bobby
Jackson, Mahalia

Jackson, Milt
Jackson, Willis
Jacquet, Illinois
Jamal, Ahmad
Jazz Crusaders
Jazz Interactions Orchestra
Jazz Messengers
Jones, Elvin
Jones, Etta
Jones, Hank
Jones, Jonah
Jones, Philly Joe
Jones, Thad
Kelly, Wynton
King, B. B.
Kirk, Roland
Lambert, Hendricks & Ross
Lateef, Yusef
Lewis, John
Lewis, Ramsey
Lloyd, Charles
Lytle, Johnny
Machito
Makeba, Miriam
Mance, Junior
Mastersounds
McCann, Les
McCoy, Freddie
McDuff, Jack
McGhee, Howard

McGriff, Jimmy
McLean, Jackie
McPherson, Charles
Mingus, Charlie
Mitchell, Blue
Mobley, Hank
Modern Jazz Quartet
Monk, Thelonious
Montgomery, Wes
Moody, James
Morgan, Lee
Morton, Jelly Roll
Newborn, Phineas
Newman, Dave "Fathead"
Parker, Charlie
Parlan, Horace
Pearson, Duke
Pepper, Art
Peterson, Oscar
Powell, Bud
Rainey, Ma
Rawls, Lou
Redd, Vi
Reed, Jimmy
Roach, Freddie
Roach, Max
Rollins, Sonny
Rushing, Jimmy
Sanders, Pharaoh
Santamaria, Mongo

Scott, Shirley
Sete, Bola
Shepp, Archie
Shorter, Wayne
Silver, Horace
Simone, Nina
Sims, Zoot
Smith, Jimmy
Smith, O. C.
Stitt, Sonny
Sun Ra
Tatum, Art
Taylor, Billy
Taylor, Cecil
Three Sounds
Timmons, Bobby
Turner, Joe
Turrentine, Stanley
Tyner, McCoy, Trio
Vaughn, Sarah
Walker, T-Bone
Waller, Fats
Washington, Dinah
Webb, Chick
Webster, Ben
Wilson, Gerald
Witherspoon, Jimmy
Young, Larry
Young, Lester